PRAY
—THE—
WORD

A Guide to Effective Praying

PRAY
—THE—
WORD

A Guide to Effective Praying

Rosalynn Nikky Adossi

PRAY THE WORD
A Guide to Effective Praying

First Edition, 2013
Copyright © 2013 Rosalynn Nikky Adossi
All rights reserved. No portion of this publication may
be reproduced without the permission of the author.
For further information contact the Author.
All scriptures in this book are from King James Version of the Bible,
New King James Version and Amplified Bible unless otherwise indicated.

ISBN: 978-0-9854723-8-2

Library of Congress Cataloging-in-Publication Data

Library of Congress Control Number: 2013952696

Edited by: Rehoboth Consultancy Service
2304 Oak Lane, 3A Ste #7,
Grand Prairie, Texas, 75051, USA
Tel: 972-742-7365,
www.rehobothbministries.org

Cover Design & Published by
Esthetic Communications
2304 Oak Lane, Suite #13
Grand Prairie, Texas, 75051, USA
www.estheticcommunications.com
Tel: (817) 659-5576

DEDICATION

This book is dedicated to the glory of the Almighty God,
the giver of life, my Lord and Savior Jesus Christ who
died for my sins to cleanse me from all unrighteousness,
and the Holy Spirit of God who is my teacher, my guide,
my paraclette, my helper and everything.
To God be the glory forever and ever, Amen.

ACKNOWLEDGMENTS

I acknowledge the influence, teachings and impartations of many men and women of God, whom I have sat under their ministries over the years. Men and women of God, who have poured into my life, and who have been of tremendous help for me in my Christian walk, but are too numerous to list in this book. I pray that God will continue to bless and uphold them.

My gratitudes also go to my family for their love and support; my darling husband Peter and my children Michael, Anne, Victor and Esther.

TABLE OF CONTENTS

PREFACE

In order to have our prayers answered we must use the language of the Spirit. Our words alone will not cut it, this is because it does not have enough power to counter the devices of the devil. The Word of God is the ammunition we need to counter every dart or arrow that the enemy might throw in our way.

I heard a man of God (Pastor Emiko Amotsuka), many years ago use the analogy of someone throwing a bullet at an object versus loading that bullet in a gun and firing it at the object. Certainly the latter action will do more damage than the former, because the impact will be felt when the bullet is shot through a gun. So also when we pray, we have to put the Word (bullet) of God in our mouth (gun) and shoot it at the enemy of our soul, the Devil. It is in that way that we will be able to stop the enemy in his tracks.

In the Bible there are many promises that God has given to those that believe in Him. Knowing the promises by reading the Bible enables us know what, and how to pray when we find ourselves in dire situations in our daily life, be it in our health, finances, relationship etc.

Do you need to pray about anything? You need to have a word for your situation. Search the Bible for a word to stand on. That is what this book seeks to achieve - that is to help bring to light some of the words of God that you can stand on regarding your situation when you pray. When you have a word to stand on regarding your situation, coupled with faith and belief in your heart, there is more boldness to look at the enemy in the face and tell him to back off!

When going through lack of peace in your life for example and you want to pray, it is important that you know what the Bible says concerning your peace. Pray that word and stand upon that word, and God is bound by His word to bring it to pass if you BELIEVE. The Bible says "He is not a man that He should lie, neither the son of man that He should repent. If He said it, will He not do it? and if He has spoken it, will He not bring it to pass?"

Speaking the Word of God in our situations has tremendous power, just as someone who puts a bullet in a gun and fires it. In the gospel of John Chapter 14:13-14 we are counseled to ask God for anything in the name of Jesus and He will do it:

> *"And whatsoever ye shall ask in my name, that will I do, that the Father may be glorified in the Son. If ye shall ask any thing in my name, I will do it." (KJV)*

It has always been my desire to have a prayer reference book that I can quickly flip through, and find the word of God that I need to stand on concerning particular situations I want to pray about. This book by no means does not list all of the promises of God in the Bible that you can stand on, but it has few listed for your reference. As you daily read the word of God and meditate on it like Joshua 1:8 promise, you will have good success, and make your way prosperous. As you read the word you will find more gems that you can put in your journal so that during your own time of prayer you will stand upon God's promises and command the Devil to bow in Jesus name! Shalom.

INTRODUCTION

Prayer is the vehicle or channel through which we communicate with our Creator, God. It is a dialogue between us and God, and it should never be a monologue. When we pray, we communicate with God. When we speak to God through our prayers, He also wants to respond by communing (Koinonia) with us. This is God's desire.

However, there are times we pray and ask for things and God does not respond immediately. This could be because His will that is expressly detailed in His Word (Bible), has not been met, or we are asking amiss. It is important, therefore that we read and meditate on the word of God so we know His will, promises, and covenant for us, so we know how to pray, and what to pray in order to possess what belongs to us. It could also be because there is sin in our lives, or unforgivingness in our heart. If you are not born again and have not given your life to Jesus, your first prayer should be God have mercy on me a sinner.

Furthermore, He wants you to come as you are, but by the time you have an encounter with Him you will never be the same again. God loves us for who we are because, He created us in His own image and likeness. But He is also a holy God and if we live an unholy life He will not hear us. All have sinned and come short of the glory of God so we need to repent and ask Him to forgive us of our sins. Until we ask for forgiveness, and also forgive those who have offended us, our prayers will not be answered. Unforgiveness in our hearts will hinder our prayers.

1

WHY DO
WE NEED TO PRAY?

T he desire of my heart has always been to let people know that it is easy for anyone to pray. Each individual who can or cannot speak can pray. Prayer can be audible or inaudible. You can pray anywhere and at anytime. Everyone and anyone can pray effectively and have their prayers answered, if they know the principles and how to apply them.

In order for us to communicate our needs to God and have our needs met daily we need to bring our request to God just like we would approach anyone that we trusted, through prayer. Philippians 4:6-7 states:

> *"Be careful for nothing; but in everything by*
> *prayer and supplication with thanksgiving let*
> *your requests be made known unto God. And the*

> *peace of God, which passeth all understanding,*
> *shall keep your hearts and minds through Christ*
> *Jesus."*

We are not to worry or fret about anything but to take them to God in prayer. Worrying about them will not solve the problem. Jeremiah 33:3 declares:

> *"Call unto me and I will show you great and*
> *mighty things that you do not know."*

When we call on God in prayer, He will show us great and mighty things that we have not previously experienced or seen. We need to pray for so many reasons: either because we need protection while we are traveling or at home, or because we need wisdom to solve a problem or make the right choice/decision.

We can pray about practically everything. Prayer can be silent or boisterous, but in order to hit your target, you have to have a word that God has given concerning that situation. You need to bring that word back to Him, and the angels of God will stand at attention to go deliver that word. This is because the angels hearken to God's word, and they are only moved by God's word. When you speak God's word, it is like God speaking, so the angels act on it.

The Word of the Lord will not return unto Him void, until it come to pass. Have faith in God and believe in your heart that He is able to do it, and He will. Hebrews 1:14 affirms that:

> *"Are not the angels all ministering spirits*
> *(servants) sent out in the service (of God for*
> *the assistance) of those who are to inherit*
> *salvation?" (Amplified Version)*

By grace we inherit salvation when we accept Jesus Christ

as our Lord and Savior. Daily living can be easy for some and complicated for others, but when we know that we have the ability to pray and ask God to intervene and help us, then the stress of daily living will be reduced or eliminated. In Matthew 7:7-8, Jesus while giving a sermon on the Mount said these words:

> *"Ask, and it shall be given you; seek, and ye shall find; knock, and it shall be opened unto you: For every one that asketh receiveth; and he that seeketh findeth; and to him that knocketh it shall be opened." (KJV)*

Sometimes we do not have our needs met because we have not asked God in prayer, we have not sought Him as we should or we have not been persistent in knocking at the door of heaven in prayer. However, it is never too late, you can start today. Matthew 7:9-11, confirms this:

> *"Or what man is there of you whom if his son ask bread, will he give him a stone? Or if he ask a fish, will he give him a serpent? If ye then, being evil, know how to give good gifts unto your children, how much more shall your Father which is in heaven give good things to them that ask him?" (KJV).*

Therefore, if we humans know how to give good gifts to our children, certainly the one who created us will give us what we ask of Him.

Sometime ago, I was about to lead prayer in a church convention, and God gave me a revelation about John 1:1-3 which says:

> *"In the beginning [before all time was the Word (Christ), and the Word was with God, and the Word was God Himself. He was present original-*

ly with God. All things were made and came into existence through him; and without Him was not even one thing made that has come into being." (Amplified Bible).

Furthermore, Colossians 1:16-17 declares that:

"For by him were all things created, that are in heaven, and that are in earth, visible and invisible, whether they be thrones, or dominions, or principalities, or powers: all things were created by him, and for him: And he is before all things, and by him all things consist."

The revelation here is that Christ is in control of principalities, powers, dominions and all things were created by him. With this revelation my faith in God soared, and it was grounded and rooted like a rock that cannot be moved. It didn't matter what it was, to me God could do anything and whatever God could not do, forget it, nobody else could do it. God can do anything, but fail. He will not fail you if you put your trust in Him.

It was my AHA moment! A light bulb went off in my head and I have never been the same since God revealed to me that Christ is God, all things were made by Him and without Him was not even one thing made that has come into being! That means if you have a need and God cannot provide it in Jesus name, it cannot be done by anybody else! He will use people to bless you, put people strategically in your path that will help you. God is able to do all things, He controls all things, and He made all things!

Even as I write, there is an excitement bubbling in my stomach knowing that God, according to Ephesians 3:20

"...is able to do exceedingly abundantly above all

that I ask or think, according to the power that works in me."

Shortly after this revelation the devil attacked me and tried to take my life. I had DVT (Deep Vein Thrombosis), on my way back from work one afternoon as I tried to drive back home. My leg was as hard as a stone, and I could not move. Needless to say someone had to take me to the hospital. This incident happened in Nigeria, and my Doctor looked at me after consulting with other doctors and said "We do not see this type of case too often. We cannot promise you anything, but you have a 50/50 chance of survival." Just then I remembered the revelation that God had given me concerning John 1:1-3, and I looked at my Doctor and told him to do what he has to do but I know my God is able to deliver me!

I recall another word of God, Isaiah 53:5 that I stood on through the period I was put on intravenous medications day and night. When I could not pray audibly, I prayed silently in the spirit. My family, friends and church family were all praying for me at this time. I had a team of doctors, and wonderful nurses who cared for me. They cared for me, but God healed me. Isaiah 53:5 says:

> *"But He was wounded for our transgressions.*
> *He was bruised for our guilt and iniquities;*
> *the chastisement [needed to obtain] peace and*
> *well-being for us was upon Him, and with the*
> *stripes (that wounded) Him we are healed and*
> *made whole." (Amplified version)*

Those words rang in my head and in my heart all day, and night during this period. I read the Word, I spoke it aloud, I believed it in faith, I received it and I appropriated it for me. The Word healed me! The Word was made flesh, and dwelt amongst us. The Word works, and Jesus is the Word!

21

Yet another word of scripture that I stood on during this period, is Psalms 118:17:

> *"I shall not die, but live, and declare the works of the Lord."*

About two weeks after, I was released from the hospital. It is important to note that I was an ordained pastor at my church at this time also, but that did not stop the devil from attacking me and wanting to kill me. He is a liar, and father of all evil!

If God healed me, He can heal you too. Nothing is too difficult for Him.

> *"For with God nothing will be impossible."*
> Luke 1:37

What is the challenge that you are facing? What is that thing in your life that you have been struggling with for years that seems insurmountable? What is that sickness, disease, or infirmity called that has been ailing you? Today is your day of salvation and deliverance for nothing is impossible with God if you have faith in His word. Ask earnestly, come in repentance forgiving those that have wronged you in life and the Lord will abundantly pardon and show you His mercy in the name of Jesus!

It is our enemy the Devil that comes to steal, kill and destroy. Christ has come to give us the abundant life in full too assure. God's plan is that we have abundance in life:- abundant joy, wealth, health, success and fulfillment in every area of our lives. John 10:10 confirms that:

> *"The thief cometh not, but for to steal, and to kill, and to destroy: I am come that they might have life, and that they might have it more abundantly." (King James Version)*

The devil does not care if you are a pastor, president, leader, king, layman or laborer, he attacks everyone all the same. You have to know the Word of God for yourself, and use it against every attack of the enemy as Ephesians 6:10-18 commands us to.

> *"Finally, my brethren, be strong in the Lord, and in the powerof his might. Put on the whole armour of God, that ye may be able to stand against the wiles of the devil. For we wrestle not against flesh and blood, but against principalities, against powers, against the rulers of the darkness of this world, against spiritual wickedness in high places. Wherefore take unto you the whole armour of God, that ye may be able to withstand in the evil day, and having done all, to stand. Stand therefore, having your loins girt about with truth, and having on the breastplate of righteousness; And your feet shod with the preparation of the gospel of peace; Above all, taking the shield of faith, wherewith ye shall be able to quench all the fiery darts of the wicked. And take the helmet of salvation, and the sword of the Spirit, which is the word of God: Praying always with all prayer and supplication in the Spirit, and watching thereunto with all perseverance and supplication for all saints;"*
> *(King James Version).*

God continues to be my healer, on several occasions I have received divine healing from the hands of the Lord whenever the enemy attacks my body, and I stand on the word. He wants us to live in divine health 365 days of the year. God is a good God.

2

HOW DO WE PRAY?

For our prayers to be effective, we have to pray to God who can solve our problems. We must pray IN THE NAME of Jesus, and in faith. Pray believing and have no doubt in your mind. Pray to the Father in Jesus' name.

> *"And whatever you ask in My name, that I will do, that the Father may be glorified in the Son. If you ask anything in My name, I will do it."*
>
> John 14:13-14

Pray in the name of Jesus Christ, ask according to the will of God and it shall be done unto you as the Bible tells us in 1 John 5:13-15:

"These things have I written unto you that believe on the name of the Son of God; that ye may know that ye have eternal life, and that ye may believe on the name of the Son of God.
And this is the confidence that we have in him, that if we ask any thing according to his will, he heareth us: And if we know that he hear us, whatsoever we ask, we know that we have the petitions that we desired of him."

Our Lord and Savior went on to say that

"...if we abide in Him and His words abide in us, we will ask what we desire, and it shall be done for us."

1 John 15:7

The effectual fervent prayer of the righteous makes tremendous power available, dynamic in its workings. When facing any circumstance, or situation we are to pray for one another as we read in James 5:13-18 which says:

"Is any among you afflicted? let him pray. Is any merry? let him sing psalms. Is any sick among you? let him call for the elders of the church; and let them pray over him, anointing him with oil in the name of the Lord: And the prayer of faith shall save the sick, and the Lord shall raise him up; and if he have committed sins, they shall be forgiven him. Confess your faults one to another, and pray one for another, that ye may be healed. The effectual fervent prayer of a righteous man availeth much. Elias was a man subject to like passions as we are, and he prayed earnestly that it might not rain: and it rained not on the earth by the space of three years and six months. And he prayed again, and the heaven gave rain, and the earth brought forth her fruit."

We cannot come to God with empty hands, just like we would not go and appear before a king empty handed. We are to appear before God with a sacrifice of our praise, thanksgiving or appreciation of who He is as we see in Psalm 100:4-5:

"Enter his gates with thanksgiving and into his courts with praise, be thankful unto him and bless his name. For the Lord is good, his mercy is everlasting, and his truth endures to all generations."

We have so much to be thankful for every day when we get up and go about our daily lives. We have need to thank God for protection, provision, favor, guidance, direction and the list goes on. We have to thank him for life itself! We are to come boldly unto the throne of grace by the blood of Jesus, because the sacrifice has been paid by him over 2000 years ago. When Jesus was in the earth over 2000 years ago his disciples asked him to teach them how to pray. In Matthew 6:9-13, He taught them to pray in this manner:

"Pray, therefore, like this: Our Father Who is in heaven, hallowed (kept holy) be Your name. Your kingdom come, Your will be done on earth as it is in heaven. Give us this day our daily bread. And forgive us our debts, as we also have forgiven (left, remitted, and let go of the debts, and have given up resentment against) our debtors. And lead (bring) us not into temptation, but deliver us from the evil one. For Yours is the kingdom and the power and the glory forever, Amen." (Amplified Version).

Offense is a great killer of any prayer life. It is important that we forgive those that offend us because if we don't, we should not expect our heavenly Father to forgive us.

Mark 11:23-26 says:

> *"For verily I say unto you, That whosoever shall say unto this mountain, Be thou removed, and be thou cast into the sea; and shall not doubt in his heart, but shall believe that those things which he saith shall come to pass; he shall have whatsoever he saith. Therefore I say unto you, what things soever ye desire, when ye pray, believe that ye receive them, and ye shall have them.*
> *And when ye stand praying, forgive, if ye have ought against any: that your Father also which is in heaven may forgive you your trespasses.*
> *But if ye do not forgive, neither will your Father which is in heaven forgive your trespasses."*

When we pray we are to acknowledge God as the Creator and giver of all good gifts. We have to desire that His will be done, and ask for what we need. Confess your sins and ask God for forgiveness of your sins and forgive those that have sinned against you, because unforgiveness in our hearts towards others will hinder our prayers. Research has shown that it causes major illnesses in the body if it is allowed to fester for a long period.

It is a negative emotion that works against the cells in the body. Scientists have discovered through studies of animals and humans alike that negative emotions are counterproductive to the well-being of the body. The Bible tells us emphatically that we have to let go of bitterness, and forgive those that have offended us or used us, and try to live at peace with all men. Sometimes the people we harbor unforgiveness against do not even know that they have offended us. So they go about enjoying life while we are seething with bitterness in our hearts, thereby opening the door to the devil to afflict us with sickness and diseases.

In addition, the element of thanksgiving is very important

in prayer also because Psalm 100:4 quoted earlier instructs us to give thanks. Giving thanks is therapeutic for the person giving it, and a blessing to the one receiving it. When the one giving knows that you appreciate what they are doing for you, they are likely to do more. The beneficiary feels a sense of gratitude for what he/she has received. We have to show God that we appreciate every little thing He does for us on a daily basis too by coming before him in thanksgiving and praise, blessing his holy name.

In conclusion, we have to pray to the Father in the name of Jesus (His Son) for our prayers to bc effective. Praise and worship God and be full of thanksgiving when you come into His presence with your needs.

3

PRAYER FOR PHYSICAL, EMOTIONAL AND INNER HEALING

The Bible declares in John 10:10 that:

> *"The thief cometh not, but for to steal, and to kill, and to destroy: I am come that they might have life, and that they might have it more abundantly."*

The devil is the thief who goes about everyday looking for who to kill, steal from and destroy either physically, or emotionally through hurts, offenses and unforgiveness. But Jesus Christ has come to give us abundant healthy life, - body, spirit and soul.

We can live in divine health because God wants us to be healthy three hundred and sixty-five (365) days of the year, nothing broken, nothing missing. The Devil is the one who attacks our bodies and our minds. God is a good God and He desires the best for us. We are the redeemed of the Lord! Christ has redeemed us from sickness, diseases, poverty by his shed blood on the cross at Calvary. We have to believe, receive this and appropriate it for our lives by making it personal, and declaring His word over our lives. We read in Galatians 3:13 that:

> *"Christ purchased our freedom (redeeming us) from the curse (doom) of the Law (and its condemnation) by (Himself) becoming a curse for us, for it is written (in the Scriptures), Cursed is everyone who hangs on a tree (is crucified)."*
> *(Amplified Version).*

When we go through pain and suffering that defies medication, that is the time to stand on the word of God. For example, we can stand on 1 Peter 2:24 and claim our healing for the wounds in our hearts, body or emotions. When we pray and have faith in God, forgive and release those individuals that might have stepped on our toes, used us, lied to us, or against us or have been mean to us, our prayers will be effective. God is faithful in that he will forgive us of any sins we might have in our lives and heal those wounds in our hearts, soul, emotions and our bodies.

In 1 Peter 2:24 we read:

> *"He personally bore our sins in His (own) body on the tree (as on an altar and offered Himself on it), that we might die (cease to exist) to sin and live to righteousness. By His wounds you have been healed." (Amplified Version).*

PRAYER:

When you pray, pray like this:

"Father, in Jesus' name, according to your Word in Isaiah 53:5:

> *"You were wounded for my transgression, bruised for my iniquities... I believe your word, and I receive it today. I appropriate your Word in my body, my situation and I declare that I am healed today because your word says so! Thank you Lord for my healing today! Amen!"*

Or pray the way you normally pray but using the above words. Make it your own, and let it be heart-felt, and God will answer you. Be fervent in prayer.

How badly do you need your healing? If you need answers to your prayers quickly, urgently and speedily, you cannot but be fervent as you pray. Believe and confess the word of God over your life, your children, your family, your finances, your marriage, your relationships, your business, your job, and every area of your life.

When we pray for healing we have to use these passages above and other healing Scriptures in the Bible, believing in our hearts and receiving the work of redemption that Christ did on Calvary. We have to believe that He died on our behalf and we can appropriate what He did on the Cross for our situation. There is no distance in prayer and when we have friends or loved ones that are far away we can still believe God for their healing, deliverance from drugs, habits that have become strongholds that they find difficult to break away from. We can believe God for what-ever needs they have in prayer and it will be answered, because Psalms 107:20 says:

> *"He sent forth his word and healed them, he rescued them from the grave".*

This connects with the request of the Centurion whose servant was sick of the palsy, and was grievously tormented. He came to Jesus that his servant be healed, and Jesus said "I will come and heal him." The Centurion now replied you do not need to come to my house, only say the word and my servant will be healed. On hearing his reply, Jesus said:

> *"Verily I say unto you, I have not found so great faith, no, not in Israel." (Matthew 8:10).*

We will receive answer to our prayers according to our faith, but we have to come to a place where we absolutely believe in our hearts that God is able to do what we ask Him in faith to do in our lives. Do you believe God today? Then ask Him for that thing you need with child like faith, and He will give you the desires of your heart in Jesus name.

We have benefits as children of God, and need to continually praise God until we receive what we are asking for. His many blessings include forgiveness of our sins, healing all our diseases, redeeming our lives from destruction, crowning us with His loving kindness, and tender mercies. He also satisfies our mouth with good things; so that our youth is renewed like the eagle's.

In Psalms 103:1-2 we are counseled to:

> *"Bless the Lord, O my soul; and all that is within me, bless his holy name. Bless the Lord, O my soul, and forget not all his benefits..."*

Continue to bless the Lord after you have prayed and believe until your manifestation comes, do not give up too soon and say it is not working or it does not work. Keep on praising and thanking the Father until you see your miracle.

You can also stand on 3rd John 1:2 on your prayer for healing. It says

> *"Beloved, I wish above all things that you prosper and be in health even as your soul prospers."*

It is clear here that it is God's will for all saints to prosper materially, in bodily healing and health as well as in their soul (to be saved from eternal damnation) and be in your right mind.

Furthermore, in Acts 10:38, we read:

> *"God anointed Jesus of Nazareth with the Holy Ghost and with power;: who went about doing good and healing all that were oppressed of the devil; for God was with him."*

Jesus Christ in Matthew 10:1:

> *"...called his twelve disciples to him, and gave them authority to drive out evil spirits and to heal every disease and sickness."*

The power has been given to the saints to heal the sick and cast out demons in the name of Jesus! Power and authority have been given to you as a believer, to lay hands on yourself, yes I said yourself! You can lay hands on yourself and command that demon to leave in Jesus name and it will obey you.

Go ahead, lay hands on yourself right now. Open your mouth and say:

"Father, according to your word in 3rd John 1:2, I prosper in my finances, I prosper in my health and my soul prospers in the mighty name of Jesus Christ I pray, Amen!

The loving expectation of God towards us is also given expression in Jeremiah 29:11:

> *"For I know the thoughts that I think toward you, saith the Lord, thoughts of peace, and not of evil, to give you an expected end." (King James version).*

There is hope in the word of God for those the Doctors have told they only have a week, a month, a year or a time frame to live. Definitely we can stand on the word, and see God perform a miracle according to our faith in Psalms 118:17:

> *"I shall not die, but live, and declare the works of the Lord." (NKJV).*

You can personalize this prayer or insert the name of the person you are praying for. For example: "Mary shall not die, but live, and declare the works of the Lord! Amen."

When Satan attacks us with sickness and diseases, we need to rise up and refuse to accept such foreign infiltrations into our bodies. Periodic illnesses are an example of this, like seasonal allergies, cold, and major ones like cancer and by whatever name they are called. We can refuse to accept these death penalties and discomforts, by uprooting them from our bodies by declaring the word of God, and commanding them to leave our bodies which is the temple of God. Jeremiah 1:10 says:

> *"See, I have this day set you over the nations and over the kingdoms, to root out and to pull down,*

to destroy and to throw down, to build and to plant."

So your prayer will be: **"I root out and pull down every symptoms of cancer cells in my body, every sinus or allergy, cold, fever or whatever the ailment is. I destroy them and throw them down in the name of Jesus. They have no power over me. I have power over them in the name of Jesus. I have the power to build and to plant therefore, I ask to be built and planted new healthy cells in my body and perfect health right now by faith in the name of Jesus! Amen. I command new cells to grow, new tissues or whatever has deteriorated in my body to be replaced by new ones in Jesus name!"**

Matthew 15:13 is another scripture that you can stand on regarding your healing. Jesus replied His disciples concerning the fact that the Pharisees were offended at what He had said:

"Every plant which My heavenly Father has not planted will be uprooted."

Sickness and diseases are not planted by God, Sometimes God allows the devil to bring sickness as in the case of Job, but they are not meant to kill us, so we can uproot them from our lives and from the lives of our loved ones.

Psalms 105:37 tells us that:

"He also brought them out with silver and gold, and there was none feeble among His tribes."

We belong spiritually to the tribes of our Lord and Savior Jesus Christ if we are born again. The Word says there was none feeble among His tribes. We can claim that for ourselves and that means none of us, our children or loved ones should be sick. We can stand on the Word of God, confess it, believe it, and declare divine health until we see the manifestation.

I am not advocating that we should not seek medical advice or take medication. Not at all, by all means see your physician and take your medications. It is God that gave the doctors wisdom for what they do. Most doctors or nurses will tell you they care for you, but it is God who heals. Sometimes we might be going through emotional stress we can stand on the word in: 2 Corinthians 4:16:

> *"Therefore we do not become discouraged (utterly spiritless, exhausted, and wearied out through fear). Though our outer man is (progressively) decaying and wasting away, yet our inner self is being (progressively) renewed day after day." (Amplified Version).*

Emotional stress sometimes is caused by the fact that we are looking at everything that is going wrong around us. When we focus on the situations in our life that seem not to be moving in the right direction, we lose hope and do not exercise faith in God. The more we focus on the problem, the bigger it gets and the smaller God gets in our thinking. The more we focus on God, and what He is able to do, the smaller the problem or challenge that we are facing gets. The following scripture is one we can stand on and believe that God will see us through.

> *"And knowing that "we walk by faith (we regulate our lives and conduct ourselves by our conviction or belief respecting man's relationship to God and divine things, with trust and holy fervor; thus we walk) not by sight or appearance."*
> 2 Corinthians 5:7

Fear is crippling and it can paralyze its victims but the word of God says in 2 Timothy 1:7:

"For God hath not given us the spirit of fear; but of power, and of love, and of a sound mind."

It pays to wait upon the Lord and allow Him to give us the strength to go through every trial and tribulation that we might experience in life. Many Christians do not have the ability to go through a test, and to be able to see at the end of the days that God is always there to see us through. We come out of tests a better person, if we are able to persevere. Romans 5:3-4 says:

> *"And not only so, but we glory in tribulations also: knowing that tribulation worketh patience; and patience, experience; and experience, hope: And hope maketh not ashamed; because the love of God is shed abroad in our hearts by the Holy Ghost which is given unto us" (KJV).*

Tough times we have heard many times don't last, but tough people do. We all go through tough times in life, but like the above scripture says, tribulation works patience in us that leads to experience, and an experience that brings hope. Hope that if God delivered you, or someone from a situation in the past, He is able to deliver you again! So, look up, He will do it again! There are tremendous benefits to waiting on the Lord as the word of God tells us in Isaiah 40:31:

> *"But those who wait on the Lord shall renew their strength, they shall mount up with wings like eagles, they shall run and not be weary, they shall walk and not faint."*

Deep emotional, spiritual and physical wounds can be healed if we stand on Jeremiah 30:17:

> *"For I will restore health unto thee, and I will heal thee of thy wounds, saith the Lord; because*

> *they called thee an Outcast, saying, This is Zion,*
> *whom no man seeketh after."*

Pray to God to heal every inner pain, and hurt if you have been abused in any way, shape or form. Hurts that are deep down in your soul can be healed by the blood of Jesus. There is a balm in Gilead, that heals the sin sick soul, and the Bible says in Jeremiah 8:22:

> *"Is there no balm in Gilead; is there no physi-*
> *cian there? Why then is not the health of the*
> *daughter of my people recovered?"*

Therefore there is confidence in the following scripture for surely God is able to heal us as we read in Jeremiah 7:14, but our responsibility is to ask:

> *"Heal me, O LORD, and I shall be healed; save*
> *me, and I shall be saved: for thou art my praise."*

PRAY THIS WAY: "Father, in the name of Jesus, I ask you to heal me of my emotional wounds, heal me of all the hurts and unforgiveness that I feel towards you Lord (if you are blaming God for your situation) and every other person (you can mention their names aloud) and set me free totally and completely. Help me Lord to release all the people that have hurt me or despitefully used me, give me grace to forgive them, Father. I pray that you would bless them right now and I release them of all wrong doing, in the name of Jesus, I pray! Amen!"

Believers need to know that:

> *"For though we walk in the flesh, we do not war*
> *after the flesh: (For the weapons of our warfare*
> *are not carnal, but mighty through God to the*

pulling down of strong holds;) Casting down imaginations, and every high thing that exalts itself against the knowledge of God, Bringing every thought into captivity to the obedience of Christ."

2 Corinthians 10:3-5

Our mind is being bombarded daily with thoughts and suggestions that are either positive or negative. We have the power to control what we allow to dominate our thoughts, and our minds through the word of God. There is a saying that you cannot prevent a bird from flying over your head, but you can prevent it from building a nest on your head.

We have to be proactive to guard our minds, and thoughts, and not allow negative thoughts to become strongholds in our lives because by then it is more difficult to dispel. We have to open our mouths and cast down imaginations and all thoughts that are ungodly from our lives because we cannot afford to dwell on them. We should think on things that are life giving as Philippians 4:8 tells us:

"Finally, brethren, whatever things are true, whatever things are noble, whatever things are just, whatever things are pure, whatever things are lovely, whatever things are of good report, if there is any virtue and if there is anything praiseworthy meditate on these things." (NKJV)

PRAYER

For inner healing for yourself and loved ones, pray to the Father in Jesus name and personalize this scripture in Ephesians 3:16:

"May He grant you out of the rich treasure of His glory to be strengthened and reinforced with

mighty power in the inner man by the (Holy) Spirit (Himself indwelling your innermost being and personality)."

"Almighty God, I pray that you will grant me strength in my innermost being out of the riches of your glory. Heal everywhere I hurt in Jesus name. Make right everything that is wrong with me in the name of Jesus Christ. Give me power to overcome what I am dealing with, and give me the grace to stand in times of temptation in the name of Jesus. Remove the desire or appetites for things that do not glorify your name, I pray in Jesus name. Amen."

You can pray in your own words and verbalize, or articulate exactly what you are feeling or going through and God will heal you of your wounds in Jesus name.

4

Prayer for Finances

The heart of a father is to meet the needs of his children. The desire of our Heavenly Father is to meet our needs. He does not want us to start a project and not finish it. He wants to give us a future and a hope. In Jeremiah 29:11 we read:

> *"For I know the thoughts and plans that I have for you, says the Lord, thoughts and plans for welfare and peace and not for evil, to give you hope in your final outcome." (Amplified Version).*

It is the will of God that we prosper, as the Scriptures says in 3rd John 1:2:

> *"Beloved, I wish above all things that you prosper and be in health even as your soul prospers."*

God's will is that we prosper not just in our finances, but spirit, soul and body. I have heard Papa Kenneth Hagin of blessed memory say several times that: "We are a tripartite being, we are a spirit, we have a soul and live in a body" After his departure to glory, Papa Hagin left behind a legacy of faith for believers all over the world. Provision has therefore been made by God whereby we prosper spirit, soul and body. Jesus taught this principle when He was here on earth.

In Luke 6:38 we read:

> *"Give, and it will be given to you: good measure, pressed down, shaken together, and running over will be put into your bosom. For with the same measure that you use, it will be measured back to you."*

If we desire financial blessings, we must follow the principle set in the Bible, as we give it shall be given back unto us. If we give sparingly, we will reap sparingly, but if we give bountifully, we shall also reap bountifully.

Many people who have no faith in God understand this biblical principle, and they follow it, and it works for them just as it would work for a believer in Christ. Whatever you need in your life give towards that, for whatever you respect is what you attract and you eventually walk in; but whatever you despise or hold in no regard can never impact your life and you will not be a partaker of it.

If we want to receive, we have to give. We have to sow a seed so there can be a harvest. God is our source and our hope, our trust and reliance should be on Him first before we look to other people or even to our own abilities, talents, influence, jobs, businesses or achievements. Isaiah 40:26 tells us to

"Lift up your eyes on high see! Who has created these? He who brings out their host by number and calls them all by name: through the greatness of His might and because he is strong in power, not one is missing or lacks anything."

Nothing broken, nothing missing! The will of God is that we lack nothing! Over the years, some ministers have taught that when you are poor God might be trying to teach you something, but Philippians 4:19 says:

"But my God shall supply all your needs according to His riches in glory, by Christ Jesus."

This is a prayer that Paul the apostle prayed on the church in Philippi thanking them for having given to him and to his ministry when he needed help, and that not that he sought the gift, but the fruit that abounds to their account.

As we give to God, He will surely supply all our needs according to His riches in glory, by Christ Jesus. God is our source. It is not the will of God that we should be poor or lack, but rather we are to live in abundance of all his blessings. He will supply all our needs according to His riches in glory, not according to our riches, not according to our jobs, not even our businesses, but His riches.

His blessings will make sure that all our needs are met. He provides for us, He is the one that gives us the power to get wealth, the ability, the talent that we need to break new grounds. Deuteronomy 28:1-14 talks about the blessing of God on the condition that we are obedient and carefully observe all His commandments which He has commanded.

There are laws and principles of the word in the Bible, that when we adhere to them, it will be well with us, and we will not live in poverty and lack.

The Principle of Sowing and Reaping is one of them: Give and it shall be given unto you good measure, pressed down shaken together and running over shall men give unto your bosom. When we give, we receive.

The Law of Reciprocity: when you sow, you reap, when you give, you receive; it works in the physical as well as in the spiritual realm. It is applicable to everyone that walks in it, be it Christian or someone that does not profess the faith. It will work for an unbeliever just like it will work as well for a believer in Christ Jesus. As long as the earth remains, seed time and harvest time shall not cease. This is why you see many people who are not Christians, but who are Atheist or people of other religious beliefs prosper in what they do. If they apply the principle of sowing and reaping, it will work for them also.

PRAYER

Pray like this: **"Father, in the name of Jesus, according to your word in Philippians 4:19, you supply all my needs ...Thank you Lord that all my needs are met according to your riches in glory, by Christ Jesus!"**

Notice also that the verse did not say "your wants", it says "your needs" those things that are important and necessary in our lives will be provided. The "wants" are extras. Deuteronomy 8:18 says:

> *"And you shall remember the Lord your God, for it is He who gives you power to get wealth that He may establish His covenant which He swore to your fathers, as it is this day."*

It is to our benefit to remember who gives us the power to get wealth, and humble ourselves to give honor to whom honor is due. There is a purpose for being blessed and that is SO YOU CAN BE A BLESSING TO OTHERS, not so that we can hoard the wealth, but for us to give to those in need also. Are you a good steward? When we give to others, we have the capacity to increase, but when we hold on tight to what we have, we tend to stagnate, because there is no room for more.

Many non-Christians understand this principle and they give all the time, and we find them increasing and we wonder why. Giving is not only in monetary terms, it can be through volunteering your time, possessions, experience, intellect, a word of encouragement, support etc. We all can give. We all have something to give. God is a giver as we see in Isaiah 45:11-12:

> *"Thus saith the LORD, the Holy One of Israel, and his Maker, Ask me of things to come concerning my sons, and concerning the work of my hands command ye me. I have made the earth, and created man upon it: I, even my hands, have stretched out the heavens, and all their host have I commanded."*

The Creator of heaven and earth is giving us a blank check right here and asking us to ask of Him anything, because He created it all. He is able to give us all the desires of our heart. He even gives houses you have not built! Exodus 1:21 confirms this:

> *"And it came to pass, because the midwives feared God, that he made them houses." (KJV)*

This passage is referring to the Hebrew midwives in Goshen who feared/reverenced the God of Israel, when they were told to kill the male babies as they were being delivered, they refused and allowed the babies to live. Moses was born at this time in Egypt. Because they reverenced God, He built them houses. Another translation says:

"He made them households of their own." (The Amplified Bible).

In a nutshell, the plan of God is that we might have more than enough, so that we can be able to help those in need as well as propagate the gospel of our Lord and Savior Jesus Christ. In 2 Corinthians 8:9 we read:

"For ye know the grace of our Lord Jesus Christ, that, though he was rich, yet for your sakes he became poor, that ye through his poverty might be rich."

Christ has paid the price. Living in poverty does not glorify God. He wants us to be rich. It is the love of money that is the root of all evil, not money itself. If we follow the principle laid down in the word of God, we can avoid living from paycheck to paycheck. We can live a life whereby all our needs are met and we have left over to bless our families and communities.

We are to bring one tenth of the income that God has blessed us with to the house of the Lord and watch Him multiply us and rebuke the enemy off our wallets and life. The one tenth of our income is known as tithe as we read in Malachi 3:10-12:

"Bring ye all the tithes into the storehouse, that there may be meat in mine house, and prove me now herewith, saith the LORD of hosts, if I will not open you the windows of heaven, and pour you out a blessing, that there shall not be room enough to receive it. And I will rebuke the devourer for your sakes, and he shall not destroy the fruits of your ground; neither shall your vine cast her fruit before the time in the field, saith the LORD of hosts. And all nations shall call you

blessed: for ye shall be a delightsome land, saith the LORD of hosts."

After you have obeyed this injunction in the word of God, and you have a need in the area of your finances, you can take this word to God in prayer and ask Him to rebuke the devourer which is the enemy that comes to steal, kill and destroy. You can command the devil to remove his hands from your life, your wallet and everything that concerns you. You can ask God to open the windows of heaven and pour you out a blessing everyday in the name of Jesus, and your prayers will be granted.

5

PRAYER
FOR MARRIAGES

"For this purpose a man shall leave his father, and mother and cleave to his wife and the two shall be one, therefore what God has put together, let no one put asunder"

(Mark 10:7-9 paraphrased by me).

Sometimes the issue of barrenness in a marriage can cause friction, anxiety and yet, there are promises in the word of God that we can stand on when we pray. Psalm 113:9 for example tells us:

"He maketh the barren woman to keep house, and to be a joyful mother of children. Praise ye the LORD."

God's promise in Exodus 23:26 confirms His desire to protect the fruits of every marriage:

> *"There shall nothing cast their young, nor be barren, in thy land: the number of thy days I will fulfill."*

Declare that over your marriage I receive the blessing of the Lord. Pray thus:

PRAYER

"Father, help us to have the Agape (unconditional) love towards one another, in addition to the Phileo (friendship) love and Erotic (passionate) love. Help us to build our love upon the solid foundation of the love God has towards us which is not selfish in Jesus' name."

"Father, in the name of Jesus, we declare non is barren in this family, there will be no miscarriage and this marriage is blessed in Jesus name! Amen."

Psalms 127:1a says:

> *"Unless the Lord builds the house, they labor in vain who build it;..."*

We have to see the marriage institution as a covenant between husband and wife before God. When we view it as a contract between the man and woman and exclude God, it is difficult to stand when challenges arise. Joshua 24:15 made it plain that he was determined to serve God and his entire family. *"...But as for me and my house, we will serve the Lord."*

We have to invite God into our marriage and ask Him to have absolute control in our home. When two different people come together to cohabit, there is bound to be differences, but when God is enthroned, the union cannot be broken - a three-fold cord cannot easily be broken. God is the one that instituted marriage and what He has joined together, let nobody put asunder. Mark 10:6-9 says:

> *"But from the beginning of the creation God made them male and female. For this cause shall a man leave his father and mother, and cleave to his wife; And they twain shall be one flesh: so then they are no more twain, but one flesh. What therefore God hath joined together, let not man put asunder."*

The issue of the man loving his wife is discussed in the following verses and the wife is to respect and honor the husband as the head of the family. Ephesians 5:31-33 affirms that:

> *"For this cause shall a man leave his father and mother, and shall be joined unto his wife, and they two shall be one flesh. This is a great mystery: but I speak concerning Christ and the church. Nevertheless let every one of you in particular so love his wife even as himself; and the wife see that she reverence her husband."*

The husband has to be obedient to the word of God as to how to love his wife so his prayers will not be hindered. I Peter 3:7-9:

> *"Likewise, ye husbands, dwell with them according to knowledge, giving honour unto the wife, as unto the weaker vessel, and as being heirs together of the grace of life; that your prayers be not hindered. Finally, be ye all of one mind, having compassion one of another, love as brethren, be pitiful, be courteous: Not rendering*

*evil for evil, or railing for railing: but contrari-
wise blessing; knowing that ye are thereunto
called, that ye should inherit a blessing."*

It is also important to mention that a wife has a duty to
respect the husband as we read in Ephesians 5:22-28:

*"Wives, submit yourselves unto your own hus-
bands, as unto the Lord. For the husband is the
head of the wife, even as Christ is the head of the
church: and he is the saviour of the body.
Therefore as the church is subject unto Christ, so
let the wives be to their own husbands in everything. Husbands, love your wives, even as Christ
also loved the church, and gave himself for it;
That he might sanctify and cleanse it with the
washing of water by the word, That he might
present it to himself a glorious church, not having spot, or wrinkle, or any such thing; but that
it should be holy and without blemish. So ought
men to love their wives as their own bodies. He
that loveth his wife loveth himself."*

We should pray that God will give us the grace to obey
his word and do what his word says to do concerning our
partner. Intimacy is very important in marriage and 1 Corinthians 7:1-5 says:

*"Now concerning the things whereof ye wrote
unto me: It is good for a man not to touch a
woman. Nevertheless, to avoid fornication, let
every man have his own wife, and let every
woman have her own husband. Let the husband
render unto the wife due benevolence: and
likewise also the wife unto the husband. The
wife hath not power of her own body, but the
husband: and likewise also the husband hath not
power of his own body, but the wife. Defraud ye*

*not one the other, except it be with consent for a
time, that ye may give yourselves to fasting and
prayer; and come together again, that Satan
tempt you not for your incontinency."*

To avoid fornication, adultery and temptation the husband
and wife are to fulfill their marital duties to one another.
Excuses of tiredness and having a headache for weeks on
end will only lead to a strain in the relationship. Pray that
God will help you forgive your spouse if you have been
offended in any way, and find the right time to discuss the
situation with them. We have to be quick to forgive and
not let the sun go down on our wrath. Do not go to bed
angry with your spouse. May the Lord help us to be doers
of his word and not just hearers only.

At the time of writing this book, this is my 29th year of
marriage to my husband, and I know that what the word
of God says about marriage is what will sustain any good
marriage. Sometimes it is difficult to forgive when you
perceive that the other person has been selfish, and self
centered in the marriage, but ask for the grace of God.
When external forces come against your marriage you can
stand on the word of God that says in Isaiah 54:17

*"No weapon that is formed against thee shall
prosper; and every tongue that shall rise against
thee in judgment thou shalt condemn. This is the
heritage of the servants of the LORD, and their
righteousness is of me, saith the LORD."*

No weapon formed against your marriage shall prosper in
the name of Jesus! Fight for your marriage and relationship. Stand in the place of intercession and pray Isaiah 7:7
which says:

*"Thus saith the Lord GOD, It shall not stand,
neither shall it come to pass."*

When people came against the people of God, the Bible declared that God said their schemes, and agenda will not stand. Do what you have to do to rectify any area that you have fallen short in your responsibility in the relationship, then go forth and stand your ground in prayer against demonic forces that might be trying to tear your marriage apart. Look for the need that your spouse has and as much as you can and with God's help try to meet that need. It can be emotional support, affection, intimacy, financial, or physical. Be there for one another in unity. Prefer one another. Be selfless, kind, gentle, trustworthy and dependable. Forgive your spouse.

6

PRAYERS FOR YOURSELF, YOUR CHILDREN AND FAMILY

Y ou need to know who you are in Christ Jesus. God created us in his likeness and image, and have an everlasting love for us. The love that God has towards us is an unconditional love (Agape). Even when we do not deserve to be loved, He still loves us. We do not have to perform before He loves us. Romans 8:32-34 says:

> *"He that spared not his own Son, but delivered him up for us all, how shall he not with him also freely give us all things? Who shall lay any thing to the charge of God's elect? It is God that justifieth. Who is he that condemneth? It is Christ that died, yea rather, that is risen again, who is even*

at the right hand of God, who also maketh intercession for us."

Day and night our Lord is praying for us, so we should stand in the gap for our children, family, friends and ourselves. Pray Psalm 139:13-18 over yourself:

"For You formed my inward parts; You covered me in my mother's womb. I will praise You, for I am fearfully and wonderfully made; Marvelous are Your works, And that my soul knows very well. My frame was not hidden from You, When I was made in secret, And skillfully wrought in the lowest parts of the earth. Your eyes saw my substance, being yet unformed. And in your book they all were written, The days fashioned for me, When as yet there were none of them. How precious also are Your thoughts for me, O God! How great is the sum of them! If I should count them, they would be more in number than the sand; When I awake, I am still with You."

Thank you Lord that you did not create a counterfeit! I am an original, created by the Most High God! Every feeling of inferiority complex is not of God, it is of the devil. We are unique in the way God created each of us, and are precious to Him. God loves us with an everlasting love, and his love is unconditional. It is not based on how good we are or how well we perform. Ephesians 3:19 says:

"(That you may really come) to know (practically, through experience for yourselves) the love of Christ, which far surpasses mere knowledge (without experience); that you may be filled (through all your being) unto all the fullness of God [may have the richest measure of the divine Presence, and become a body wholly filled and flooded with God Himself]!" (Amplified Version)

Pray that God will open your eyes of understanding that you may know the hope of his calling as declared in Ephesians 1:17-19:

> *"That the God of our Lord Jesus Christ, the Father of glory, may give unto you the spirit of wisdom and revelation in the knowledge of him: The eyes of your understanding being enlightened that ye may know what is the hope of his calling, and what the riches of the glory of his inheritance in the saints, And what is the exceeding greatness of his power toward us who believe, according to the working of his mighty power."*

This is a prayer that I pray for myself everyday personalizing it because I realize I need God's guidance, wisdom and revelation. Your calling could be in business, politics, banking, ministry, social worker, working with children, medical field, engineering field, whatever field God has called you and given you a passion for, you need for God to give you the spirit of wisdom and revelation for.

We have all been called to share the gospel in our different sphere of life and calling, so wherever you find yourself be the epistle that can be read by all men and let them see the glory of God radiate in your life. Let your light shine wherever you are. Be an ambassador for Christ. Pray that God open your eyes to the treasures that He has already attached your name, to which sometimes we are not aware of either because we are not in the right place at the right time or we are not doing what we are supposed to be doing.

We might be overwhelmed or frustrated that things are not going the way we expect them to go, that is the right time to pray that God open my eyes of understanding to see the hope of your glory. Have faith in God. Believe His Word, read and meditate the word of God, so you know what belongs to you in Christ Jesus. Claim the promises of God and walk in total victory today. Claim the blessings of God for your life in Deut. 28:1-14 as you are careful to obey the commandments of God and walk in his ways daily. The Bible says:

> *"It will come to pass if you diligently obey the voice of the Lord:"*
>
> Deut. 28:1

Among the blessings promised to the believer in Deuteronomy 28:1-14 are:-

1. God will set you high above all nations of the earth (this refers to the Jews but believers in Christ Jesus are spiritual Israelites)
2. Blessings will come upon you and overtake you.
3. Blessed in the city and in the country
4. Blessed will be the fruit of your body (children), and whatever your trade is or where you work.
5. Blessed will be your finances, you will not lack.
6. Blessed when you come in and when you go out, God's divine protection over your life.
7. Your enemies will be defeated who rise up against you. When they come one way, they will flee seven ways because they will be utterly defeated.
8. Your bank account will be blessed and everything you put your hands to do, ideas, start-ups will prosper.
9. He will bless you in the land which he is giving you. Geographical location will not be a hindrance to your blessing
10. He will establish you a holy people to Himself, just as He has sworn to you, if you keep His commandment and walk in His ways
11. He will prosper you in every area of life.
12. You will lend to nations and not borrow.
13. He will make you the head and not the tail, above only and not beneath, etc.

The condition is you have to obey the word of the Lord and keep his commandment. Not to go after other gods or turn away from serving God. If we do our part, God is faithful to do His part. And right after those verses to the end of the chapter is the reward for disobedience.

The Bible lets us know that if we teach our children the way of the Lord when they are young great will be their peace. Pray Isaiah 54:13 over your children: *"All your children shall be taught by the LORD, And great shall be the peace of your children."*

We have the responsibility to teach our children the way of the Lord from when they are little. Teach them by sowing the seed of righteousness in their lives when they are young and you will reap the harvest when they grow up.

Psalm 37:25 says:

> *"I have been young, and now am old; Yet I have not seen the righteous Forsaken, Nor his descendants begging bread."*

We can teach our children early to trust God, depend on Him and follow the principles set for us in the word of God. When the book does not depart from their mouth and they meditate on it day and night they will end up prosperous and have good success as Joshua 1:8 tells us

> *"This book of the Law shall not depart from your mouth, but you shall meditate in it day and night, that you may observe to do according to all that is written in it. For then you will make your way prosperous, and then you will have good success."*

Children are precious gifts from the Lord. No child is a mistake, regardless of the circumstance of their birth. God has a plan and a purpose for every child. Psalms 127:3-5 says:

> *"Lo, children are an heritage of the LORD: and the fruit of the womb is his reward. As arrows are in the hand of a mighty man; so are children of the youth. Happy is the man that hath his quiver full of them: they shall not be ashamed, but they shall speak with the enemies in the gate." (KJV)*

When children are disobedient and acting contrary to the way you have raised them, you must continue to pray a blessing over their lives and speak those things that you desire to see come to pass in their lives. It is hard to speak things we do not see, but we have to discipline ourselves to speak life over our children. Deuteronomy 5:16 says:

> *"Honour thy father and thy mother, as the LORD thy God hath commanded thee; that thy days may be prolonged, and that it may go well with thee, in the land which the LORD thy God giveth thee."*

PRAYER FOR YOUR CHILDREN

Pray the following list of requests for your children

1. "Father in the name of Jesus, my children will honor their parents, as God has commanded. They will live long and it will be well with them wherever they live. They will be fruitful and multiply wherever they are to the glory of God. Amen.

2. Break the spirit of rebellion and stubbornness off of the lives of your children, and plead the blood of Jesus to cover their minds, and that God will deliver them

from every yoke of bondage. I Samuel 15:23a says:

> *"For rebellion is as the sin of witchcraft, and stubbornness is as iniquity and idolatry."*

Christ has redeemed us and our children by His blood as we read in Galatians 3:13:

> *"Christ hath redeemed us from the curse of the law, being made a curse for us: for it is written, Cursed is every one that hangeth on a tree:"* *(KJV)*

3. Declare and decree that your children are redeemed by the blood of Jesus. Declare they have the mind of Christ. I Corinthians 2:16 says:

> *"For who hath known the mind of the Lord, that he may instruct him? But we have the mind of Christ."*

4. Ask the anointing of God to destroy every yoke and remove every burden in their lives in Jesus name. Isaiah 10:27:

> *"And it shall come to pass in that day, that his burden shall be taken away from off thy shoulder, and his yoke from off thy neck, and the yoke shall be destroyed because of the anointing."*

5. Pray your children will be as the sons of Issachar who knew the signs of the times. I Chronicles 12:32:

> *"Of the sons of Issachar who had understanding of the times, to know what Israel ought to do, their chiefs were two hundred; and all their brethren were at their command."*

6. Ask God to give your children the Spirit of discernment to see far, to see things that are invisible to the naked eye.

7. Pray that God will give them wisdom and understanding to know what to do at the right time in their lives, that they will neither procrastinate, nor get involved with negative influencers.

8. Ask God to number their days, be conscious of time and apply their hearts unto wisdom.

9. Pray that they will rebuild and bring life back to whatever is good and has become stagnant in the family. Isaiah 61:4

> *"And they shall rebuild the old ruins, They shall raise up the former desolations, And they shall repair the ruined cities, the desolations of many generations."*

10. Pray that God will restore whatever has been stolen from you or your family according to the word of God in. Joel 2:25-26 which says,

> *"So I will restore to you the years that the swarming locust has eaten, the crawling locust, the consuming locust, and the chewing locust, my great army which I sent among you.*
> *You shall eat in plenty and be satisfied, and praise the name of the Lord your God, who has dealt wondrously with you; and my people shall never be put to shame."*

11. Pray for their protection. God is the protection for your family. While they are with you, away from you, in school, at work, driving, walking, flying or wherever

they go, He wants to watch over you and your loved ones. Psalm 91 says:

> *"He that dwelleth in the secret place of the most High shall abide under the shadow of the Almighty. I will say of the LORD, He is my refuge and my fortress: my God; in him will I trust. Surely he shall deliver thee from the snare of the fowler, and from the noisome pestilence. He shall cover thee with his feathers, and under his wings shalt thou trust: his truth shall be thy shield and buckler. Thou shalt not be afraid for the terror by night; nor for the arrow that flieth by day; Nor for the pestilence that walketh in darkness; nor for the destruction that wasteth at noonday. A thousand shall fall at thy side, and ten thousand at thy right hand; but it shall not come nigh thee. Only with thine eyes shalt thou behold and see the reward of the wicked. Because thou hast made the LORD, which is my refuge, even the most High, thy habitation; There shall no evil befall thee, neither shall any plague come nigh thy dwelling. For he shall give his angels charge over thee, to keep thee in all thy ways. They shall bear thee up in their hands, lest thou dash thy foot against a stone. Thou shalt tread upon the lion and adder: the young lion and the dragon shalt thou trample under feet. Because he hath set his love upon me, therefore will I deliver him: I will set him on high, because he hath known my name. He shall call upon me, and I will answer him: I will be with him in trouble; I will deliver him, and honour him. With long life will I satisfy him, and shew him my salvation." (KJV)*

We are hedged in and protected by the mighty hand of God

according to His word in Psalm 139:5 *"You have hedged me behind and before, and laid your hand upon me."*

12. A prayer that we can pray for our children's protection any day is in Psalm 23:1-6:,

> *"The Lord is my shepherd; I shall not want.
> He makes me to lie down in green pastures,
> He leads me beside the still waters. He restores
> my soul, He leads me in the paths of righteous-
> ness for his name's sake. Yea, though I walk
> through the valley of the shadow of death, I
> will fear no evil; for You are with me, Your rod
> and Your staff, they comfort me. You prepare a
> table before me in the presence of my enemies;
> You anoint my head with oil; My cup runs over.
> Surely goodness and mercy shall follow me all
> the days of my life; and I will dwell in the house
> of the Lord forever."*

13. Pray for increase over your children using 1 Chronicles 4:10 which says:

> *"And Jabez called on the God of Israel saying,
> "Oh, that You would bless me indeed, and
> enlarge my territory, that Your hand would be
> with me, and that You would keep me from evil,
> that I may not cause pain" So God granted him
> what he requested."*

14. Pray this over your children daily because you fear (reverence) and delight in the commandments of the Lord. Pray that your children and grandchildren will be great in life, they will know and serve God and be blessed.

> *"His descendants will be mighty on earth; The
> generation of the upright will be blessed."*
>
> Psalms 112:2

Prayer over your family is essential to see the hands of God move mightily in your life.

15. Pray that your children will serve the Lord all the days of their lives. Joshua said *"...as for me and my house we will serve the Lord."* Josh 24:15b

Break any demonic stronghold in your family and all generational curses in Jesus name. How do you know there is a demonic stronghold in the family? When there is a pattern of failure, sickness, addiction, death or negative behavior that runs from one generation in the family to the next, you know there is a stronghold. An example is when people die at a young age all the time in that family. Or there is a particular sickness that attacks members of the family, and grandpa might have died from it, so did aunt Betty and now cousin Jake is sick with that same disease, you know it runs in the family and has to be broken in Jesus name. Psalms 124:1-8 says:

> *"If it had not been the LORD who was on our side, now may Israel say; If it had not been the LORD who was on our side, when men rose up against us: Then they had swallowed us up quick, when their wrath was kindled against us: Then the waters had overwhelmed us, the stream had gone over our soul: Then the proud waters had gone over our soul. Blessed be the LORD, who hath not given us as a prey to their teeth. Our soul is escaped as a bird out of the snare of the fowlers: the snare is broken, and we are escaped. Our help is in the name of the LORD, who made heaven and earth."*

Open your mouth and declare that Father, in the name of Jesus Christ every demonic stronghold in my family is broken, every attack is rendered useless, our soul is escaped from the snare of the devil and we are set free and delivered in the name of Jesus! Amen.

Colossians 1:9-13 says:

> *"For this cause we also, since the day we heard*
> *it, do not cease to pray for you, and to desire that*
> *ye might be filled with the knowledge of his will*
> *in all wisdom and spiritual understanding;*
> *That ye might walk worthy of the Lord unto all*
> *pleasing, being fruitful in every good work, and*
> *increasing in the knowledge of God;*
> *Strengthened with all might, according to his*
> *glorious power, unto all patience and longsuffer-*
> *ing with joyfulness; Giving thanks unto the*
> *Father, which hath made us meet to be partakers*
> *of the inheritance of the saints in light:*
> *Who hath delivered us from the power of dark-*
> *ness, and hath translated us into the kingdom*
> *of his dear Son:"*

Pray the Aaronic blessing over your children. God told Moses to ask Aaron to pray this blessing over the children of Israel and since as a believer, we are spiritual Israelites, this blessing belongs to us too. In Numbers 6:24-26:

> *"The LORD bless thee, and keep thee: The*
> *LORD make his face shine upon thee, and be*
> *gracious unto thee: The LORD lift up his counte-*
> *nance upon thee, and give thee peace."*

PRAYER

Pray, **"Father in the name of Jesus, I ask that you give me peace, fill me, my children and grandchildren with knowledge of your will in all wisdom and spiritual understanding. Help me to walk worthy of you O God,**

fruitful in every good work and increasing in knowledge of you."

Turn the word of God into prayer, pray the word always during your prayer time or your family prayer time, in the midst of friends or a group of people. The purpose of God is that we live long so that we can fulfill the destiny that God has for us.

Pray the following prayers in Psalms 91:16 over yourself, your children and family:

> *"With long life will I satisfy him, and shew him my salvation."*

Pray also Isaiah 28:18a:

> *"And your covenant with death shall be disannulled, and your agreement with hell shall not stand;"*

Every covenant with death and agreement with the grave that we might have made out of ignorance, or our parents or anyone has made on our behalf without our knowledge shall not stand in the name of Jesus! Every attack of the enemy against us shall not stand the Bible tells us. Attacks in our dreams, verbally or through any means will surely fail. Isaiah 7:7 says:

> *"Thus saith the Lord GOD, It shall not stand, neither shall it come to pass."*

We are covered by the BLOOD of Jesus Christ and we have been redeemed by the shed blood of Jesus Christ. There are times when you have prayed, God has healed you and you have seen the manifestation of your healing and are rejoicing, but days, weeks or months down the road you start feeling the same symptoms that you felt before you became sick. Do not accept the lie of the devil! Do not be silent and tolerate the pain or symptoms. Open your mouth and declare the word of the Lord in Nahum 1:9:

> *"What do ye imagine against the LORD? He will make an utter end: affliction shall not rise up the second time."*

If God has healed you at any time and the Devil is trying to bring back the symptoms or whispering to your ear that you were not really healed, open your mouth and pray that affliction will not return a second time in the name of Jesus.

Do you have heart tremors or heart problems, you can stand on the word in Psalms 112:8:

> *"His heart is established, he shall not be afraid, until he see his desire upon his enemies."*

Pray, **"Father in the name of Jesus, my heart is steady and established and I am not afraid. Are you troubled in any way, shape or form? What is that thing in your life or the life of your loved ones that refuses to change and you have done all that you know how to do and still there is no solution. What is the "cause" of your sleeplessness, depression, oppression or has taken your joy today. Confront that problem in the name of the Lord!"**

We read In 1 Samuel 17:29.

> *"And David said, What have I now done? Is there not a cause?"*

1 Samuel 17:45:

> *"Then said David to the Philistine, Thou comest*

70

to me with a sword, and with a spear, and with a shield: but I come to thee in the name of the LORD of hosts, the God of the armies of Israel, whom thou hast defied."

This is the story of David and Goliath, where Goliath defied the armies of Israel for days and David took it personally and wanted the reproach to be removed. He called upon the name of the Lord because there was a "cause" for him to be angry at what Goliath was saying against the people of Israel and challenging them in battle. Whatever our "cause" is that the enemy of our soul is defying, we need to rise up like David did with a holy anger and come against the devil *"...in the name of the LORD of hosts, the God of the armies of Israel"*

What is your "cause" today? Arise and speak forth the word of God.

7

BREAK-THROUGH PRAYERS

It is the will of God for us to prosper. There are times that we need a job, a promotion, or we need something to change in our lives. We might need the favor of God to give us that victory that we seek that has eluded us for a long time. Please find itemized below strategic prayer points for various areas of need. Let us begin with prayer of favor.

1. Favor: We need to pray Psalms 102:13:

> *"You will arise and have mercy on Zion; for the time to favor her, yes the set time, has come".*

Pray, **"Lord, arise and have mercy on me, for the time**

to favor me, yes the set time has come in the name of Jesus!" Zion is the Church of the living God and if you are a born again child of God, that applies to you.

You can also pray:

"Father in Jesus name arise and have mercy on me, for the time to favor me has come and it is now. I thank you that your favor is upon me even as I go for this interview, assessment or whatever it is you believe God for."

2. Divine Access: When we need doors to be opened for us in order to have access to those in authority, to have a contract or loan approved, promotion, increase, favor, enlargement of our coast, we can stand on the word in John 10:9:

> "I am the door, if anyone enters by Me, he will be saved, and will go in and out and will be saved" (NKJV).

God is able to open unto us doors of opportunity, promotion and favor that no one can shut. Even when we do not have the influence or clout to get ahead, God can make a way. Revelations 3:8 says:

> "I know thy works: behold, I have set before thee an open door, and no man can shut it: for thou hast a little strength, and hast kept my word, and hast not denied my name." (KJV)

Your prayer point will be: **"Lord God, I acknowledge you as the Door, I ask that you grant me access into the breakthrough that I need (you can specifically name the area you are praying about).**

3. Dislodging Satanic Roadblocks: There are times we

see roadblocks in our journey in life and it seems that nothing is happening or we are unable to move forward. This was a situation the children of Israel faced in Egypt when God asked Moses to perform some miracle before Pharaoh so he can let the children of Israel go and worship Him.

In Exodus 8:18 we read:

> *"Now the magicians so worked with their en-chantments to bring forth lice, but they could not. So there were lice on man and beast. Then the magicians said to Pharaoh, "This is the finger of God." But Pharaoh's heart grew hard, and he did not heed them, just as the Lord had said."*

We see that the magicians tried their magic, but it did not work and only the miracle of God prevailed; and in some circumstances in our journey in life we need the miracle of God to see us through.

You will pray: **"Lord God, in the name of Jesus let your finger remove and annihilate every work of Satan in my life, or situation, so that all eyes will see that the Finger of God prevail in my case!"**

4. Dealing with the Mountains of Prey: In order to move into our purpose in life, most times we need others to come alongside of us and help us. We can ask obstacles and mountains blocking our way to success and progress be moved in Jesus name as in Zechariah 4:5-9:

> *"Then the angel that talked with me answered and said unto me, knowest thou not what these be? And I said, No, my lord. Then he answered and spake unto me, saying, This is the word of the LORD unto Zerubbabel, saying, Not by might, nor by power, but by my spirit, saith the*

LORD of hosts. Who art thou, O great mountain? before Zerubbabel thou shalt become a plain: and he shall bring forth the headstone thereof with shoutings, crying, Grace, grace unto it. Moreover the word of the LORD came unto me, saying, The hands of Zerubbabel have laid the foundation of this house; his hands shall also finish it; and thou shalt know that the LORD of hosts hath sent me unto you."

Pray that **every mountain in your path be made plain in the name of Jesus and whatever you have started you will finish in the name of Jesus. "Let your double grace prevail in my life in Jesus name."**

5. Destiny Helpers: We need destiny helpers to help bring to manifestation that which God has ordained in our lives. We read in 2 Corinthians 1:24:

"Not that we have dominion over your faith, but are fellow workers for your joy; for by faith you stand."

Our prayer should be:

"Father, in the name of Jesus send my destiny helpers, to help fulfill the call or assignment that you have given me, my children and my family. Send me those that will stand with me in faith, guidance, finances and every way I need help to fulfill my destiny in Jesus name."

6. Victory in the Midst of Trials: Declare your victory in the midst of trials and tribulations, for we walk by faith and not by sight. For the things we see are temporary and subject to change, but the things that are unseen are eternal. In 1 Samuel 17:26-37, we read the story of David and Goliath and how David put his faith in the God of Israel who had delivered him in the past from the lion and the bear while he watched his father's sheep. We see David in this passage declaring his victory in the midst of battle that looked impossible to win. So also, we have to learn to see the end from the beginning, and realize that greater is He that is in us, than he that is in the world.

The greater One in us will always put us over every obstacle, trial and tribulation in life if we learn to put our focus on Him and not on our challenges. Isaiah 41:18 says:

> *"I will open rivers in high places, and fountains in the midst of the valleys: I will make the wilder ness a pool of water, and every dry land springs of water."*

7. Rivers of Blessings: You cannot see this except you look at your situation with the eye of faith. Pray:

"Father open rivers of your blessing over my life, remove every dry place in my life that is not yielding fruit and make it springs of water, make me fruitful and full of success in Jesus name."

8. Open Doors of Blessings: In Revelation 3:7-8 we read:

> *"And to the angel of the church in Philadelphia write; These things saith he that is holy, he that is true, he that hath the key of David, he that openeth, and no man shutteth; and shutteth, and no man openeth; I know thy works: behold, I have set before thee an open door, and no man can shut it: for thou hast a little strength, and hast kept my word, and hast not denied my name". (KJV)*

God has opened doors of blessing and miracles unto us that no man can shut.

8

DELIVERANCE PRAYERS

D eliverance is needed for anyone bound by anything that has become a stronghold that is difficult to break free from. Addictions of any form qualify for a need for deliverance. The name and the blood of Jesus is what brings deliverance as we read in Philippians 2:10:

> *"That at the name of Jesus every knee should bow, of things in heaven, and things in earth, and things under the earth;"*

Hebrews 12:24 also declares:

> *"And to Jesus the mediator of the new covenant, and to the blood of sprinkling, that speaketh better things than that of Abel."*

You need deliverance for barrenness, poverty, substance abuse, alcohol, sickness, diseases, destructive way of life that runs in a family from one generation to another. After deliverance, it is important to remain in the Lord, avoid those people or situations that encourage that lifestyle. Keep up your confession of faith.

Curses could elicit short life span for its victims, where people do not live long in a family over a certain number of years; that family needs deliverance and 2 Corinthians 10:5 says:

> *"Casting down imaginations, and every high thing that exalteth itself against the knowledge of God, and bringing into captivity every thought to the obedience of Christ;"*

God is our deliverer and when we cry out to Him, He hears us. King David in the Bible was a man that knew how to quickly run to God for help when in trouble and we see this also in Psalm 61:1 where he says:

> *"Hear my cry, O God; attend unto my prayer, from the end of the earth will I cry unto thee, when my heart is overwhelmed; lead me to the rock that is higher than I." (KJV)*

Jesus Christ is the Rock of Ages; He is that Rock that we can run to and we will be safe. Jesus Christ came that He might destroy the works of the devil, which is sin and every work of darkness; as we read in 1 John 3:8:

> *"He who sins is of the devil, for the devil has sinned from the beginning. For this purpose the Son of God was manifested, that He might destroy the works of the devil."*

1. Deliverance from the Mighty: There are times we are confronted or being weighed down by those that are mightier than us either in position, authority or in other areas. It looks like we are no match for them and we are utterly overwhelmed. When people oppress us the Lord will fight for us. The Bible says in Isaiah 49:24-25 that:

"Shall the prey be taken from the mighty, or the captives of the righteous be delivered? But thus says the Lord; "Even the captives of the mighty shall be taken away, and the prey of the terrible be delivered; for I will contend with him who contends with you, and I will save your children."

Amen in the name of Jesus Christ! God will contend with those who contend with us and deliver us from their plots. He will deliver us from those that oppress us in any way, shape or form. God will deliver the weak from the strong. When evil doers are bent on destroying your reputation, you can be rest assured that God will come to your aid if you cry out to Him, for Isaiah 44:25 says:

"Who frustrates the signs of the babblers, and drives diviners mad; who turns wise men backward, and makes their knowledge foolishness;"

The Prayer point is: **"Father, in the name of Jesus frustrate every imagination of the wicked against me and bring them to nothing! Let every negative word they say against me be null and void and of no effect in the name of Jesus. Frustrate their agenda O Lord!"**

2. Deliverance from Evil Weapons: When people plot or connive together against us we can also stand on the Word and pray Isaiah 54:15-17 which says:

"Indeed they shall surely assemble, but not because of Me. Whosoever assembles against you shall fall for your sake. Behold, I have created the blacksmith who blows the coals in the fire,

who brings forth an instrument for his work,
and I have created the spoiler to destroy.
No weapon formed against you shall prosper,
and every tongue which rises against you in
judgment you shall condemn. This is the heritage
of the servants of the Lord, and their righteous-
ness is of Me."

Pray: **"Father, in the name of Jesus no weapon formed or fashioned against me shall prosper and every tongue that rises up in judgment against me I condemn right now because this is my heritage and my righteousness is of the Lord! He fights for me and I hold my peace."**

3. Deliverance from Evil Spirits: The Lord, Jesus Christ said whatever we bind on earth will be bound in heaven, so we have the power to bind those spirits that is behind the gossip, malice and backbiting and render them power-less in Jesus name. Matthew 18:18 declares:

> *"Assuredly, I say to you, whatever you bind on earth will be bound in heaven, and whatever you loose on earth will be loosed in heaven."*

4. Wall of Fire Round About: Pray that the Lord will build a wall of fire round about you that the enemy cannot penetrate as in Zachariah 2:5 which says

> *"For I; says the Lord, will be a wall of fire all around her, and I will be the glory in her midst."*

5. Stability in God: Pray that as you trust in the Lord you shall not be moved and God will surround you and your family as the mountains is round about Jerusalem, for the punishment of the wicked will not be the lot of the righteous in Jesus name. Psalms 125:1-3 says:

> *"They that trust in the LORD shall be as mount*

*Zion, which cannot be removed, but abideth for
ever. As the mountains are round about Jerusalem, so the LORD is round about his people from
henceforth even for ever. For the rod of the wicked shall not rest upon the lot of the righteous; lest
the righteous put forth their hands unto iniquity."
(KJV)*

6. Let God Arise: God fought for the children of Israel in
the Old Testament and He has not stopped fighting for His
children today. We can stand on His word and expect Him
to fight for us as Deut 1:30 says:

> *"The Lord your God, who goes before you, He
> will fight for you, according to all He did for you
> in Egypt before your eyes," (NKJV).*

When nations rose up against the people of God they were
reassured that the plans of the enemy will come to naught.
In Isaiah 7:6-7 we read:

> *"Let us go up against Judah and trouble it, and
> let us make a gap in its wall for ourselves, and
> set a king over them, the son of Tabel" – thus
> says the Lord GOD; "It shall not stand, nor shall
> it come to pass."*

Pray: **"Father in the name of Jesus! Every attack of the
enemy against me shall not stand and every evil plan
against me or my children shall not come to pass."**

7. Total Dependence on God: We have to acknowledge
in the midst of our trials and tribulations that God is our
helper and our strength. Our total dependence should be
on Him and our heart must trust Him absolutely that He
alone has all the power to deliver us. Psalms 28:7 says:

> *"The Lord is my strength and my shield; my*

heart trusted in Him, and I am helped; therefore my heart greatly rejoices, and with my song I will praise Him." (NKJV).

It is not easy to praise when we are going through a trial or tribulation, but when we do, we are saying in a loud voice to ourselves, to the Devil and to God that we trust God to deliver us and we have faith that He will do what He says He will do in our lives. When we pray for deliverance for ourselves, our children, family members or are praying for people, we want them to be delivered spirit, soul and body. God is our defense. Psalms 124:1-8 says:

"If it had not been the Lord who was on our side, Let Israel now say; If it had not been the Lord who was on our side, when men rose up against us, Then they would have swallowed us alive, when their wrath was kindled against us; Then the waters would have overwhelmed us, the stream would have gone over our soul; Then the swollen waters would have gone over our soul." Blessed be the Lord, who has not given us as prey to their teeth.
Our soul has escaped as a bird from the snare of the fowlers, The snare is broken, and we have escaped. Our help is in the name of the Lord, who made heaven and earth."

The SNARE OF THE ENEMY IS BROKEN and WE HAVE ESCAPED!

8. Stand on the Word for Victory: Stand on the Word, declare it over and over and trust God for your deliverance in Jesus name!!You are untouchable and the enemy cannot touch you or your loved ones because you bear the marks of Christ. Galatians 6:17 says:

"From henceforth let no man trouble me: for I bear in my body the marks of the Lord Jesus."

Pray: **"Father, in the name of Jesus Christ, from henceforth let no man, woman, demons or the devil trouble me: for I bear in my body the marks of the Lord Jesus! I am covered by the blood of Jesus!**

Colossians 1:20 tells us that:

"And, having made peace through the blood of his cross, by him to reconcile all things unto himself; by him, I say, whether they be things in earth, or things in heaven."

9. Plead the Blood of Jesus: It is the blood of Jesus that delivers, and heals us of all infirmities, diseases, sicknesses, bondages, negative habits that have become strongholds. Total deliverance comes from faith in the shed blood of Jesus Christ done on your behalf and my behalf. Accept by faith the finished work on the cross at Calvary today and be made whole in the name of Jesus!

9

DIFFERENT TYPES OF PRAYER

PRAYER OF INTERCESSION

This is a prayer you say on behalf of someone else. It is done when you are asked to pray, or you have the urge to do so for another person. It is an unselfish prayer, and God is looking for someone to stand in the gap for our leaders, countries, neighbor, friends, co-workers, family, and for unsaved souls all over the world so that He can show mercy as we read in 1 Timothy 2:1:

> *"I exhort therefore, that, first of all, supplications, prayers, intercessions, [and] giving of thanks, be made for all men;"*

Jesus Christ is our perfect example. He is at the right hand of the Father interceding on our behalf day and night.

Romans 8:27, and 34 tells us:

> *"And he that searcheth the hearts knoweth what is the mind of the Spirit, because he maketh intercession for the saints according to the will of God."*

> *"Who is he that condemneth? It is Christ that died, yea rather, that is risen again, who is even at the right hand of God, who also maketh intercession for us."*

We are further informed in Hebrews 7:25 that our Savior ever lives to make intercession for us:

> *"Wherefore he is able also to save them to the uttermost that come unto God by him, seeing he ever liveth to make intercession for them."*

May I inform you that love is the foundation for successful prayer. This is because as Roman 5:5 tells us. *"...the love (agape-unconditional love) of God is shed abroad in our hearts by the Holy Ghost which is given unto us."*

Someone once said "love is the basis for all Christian activity." Compassion is an ingredient of divine love. Jesus had compassion on the sick. The most effective prayer is the prayer the Holy Spirit inspires which is needed at the moment because He knows the mind of God and He will help us to pray. Ephesians 6:18 tells us to

> *"...pray always with all prayer and supplication in the Spirit, and watching thereunto with all perseverance and supplication for all saints."*

We are therefore to intercede for others, even as Ezekiel 22:30-31 is still searching for men who stand in the gap:

"And I sought for a man among them, that should make up the hedge, and stand in the gap before me for the land, that I should not destroy it: but I found none"

God is looking for someone always to stand in the gap. We are to stand in the gap for a person, persons or a nation to hold back judgment. It is most effective when prompted by the Holy Spirit. In Genesis 18:16-33 we see for example, Abraham intercede for his nephew Lot. In verses 20, and 21 of that same chapter it says *"...a cry arose out of Sodom."*

Smith Wigglesworth said **"that there is something about faith that will cause God to pass over a million people just to get to one person who is in faith".** The cry of faith calls forth or put into operation, a blessing from God.

2 Chronicles 7:14 says:

"If my people, which are called by my name, shall humble themselves, and pray, and seek my face, and turn from their wicked ways; then will I hear from heaven, and will forgive their sin, and will heal their land."

This confirms the desire of God in Ezekiel 22:30,31 that God is still looking for someone to stand in the gap, to intercede on the behalf of other people so He can meet needs, forgive their sins, give them a second, third, fourth, fifth or whatever chance they need to get back on their feet. The will of God is for people to turn unto him, choose life and live.

Our Lord is our Intercessor as we see in 1 Timothy 2:5:

"For there is one God, and One Mediator between God and men, the man Christ Jesus."

Hebrews 7:25 also gives us the confidence by saying that:

> *"Wherefore he is able also to save them to the uttermost that come unto God by him, seeing He ever liveth to make intercession for them."*

There is a reward for standing in the gap and interceding for others as we read in Isaiah 53:12:

> *"Therefore will I divide him [a portion] with the great, and he shall divide the spoil with the strong; because he hath poured out his soul unto death: and he was numbered with the transgressors; and he bare the sin of many, and made intercession for the transgressors."*

I am a living witness of this. For many years my husband and I have diligently served in the Prison Ministry, fed and clothed the poor in Homeless Shelters, and we have seen God bless our family beyond our wildest dreams.

PRAYER OF AGREEMENT

This is a prayer by two or more people. God has given us the power to bind and loose and He promised that where two or three are gathered in His name, He will be there in their midst. In Mathew 18:18-20 we read:

> *"Verily I say unto you, Whatsoever ye shall bind on earth shall be bound in heaven: and whatsoever ye shall loose on earth shall be loosed in heaven. Again I say unto you, That if two of you shall agree on earth as touching any thing that they shall ask, it shall be done for them of my Father which is in heaven. For where two or three are gathered together in my name, there am I in the midst of them."*

Look for someone that believes the word of God, who has no doubt in their mind about what God is saying concerning your situation and agree with them in prayer. Your spouse, family members, church members or colleagues at work who are believers. However, make sure they are not tail bearers also, so that your business will not be the talk of your community. Make sure they are people that are trustworthy.

Joshua 23:10 tells us:

> *"One man of you shall chase a thousand: for the LORD your God, he it is that fighteth for you, as he hath promised you."*

One of us when we pray shall put to flight a thousand of the agents of the devil because God is with us and two of us shall put to flight ten thousand: that is the mathematics of God. Our joint prayers in agreement will destroy the camp of the enemy in Jesus name!

Deuteronomy 32:30 declares to us:

> *"How should one chase a thousand, and two put ten thousand to flight, except their Rock had sold them, and the LORD had shut them up?"*

Victory is sure because God has given the enemy into our hands and paralyzed all their works against us when we touch in agreement, and pray concerning anything.

PRAYER OF THANKSGIVING

A prayer of appreciation of what God has done for you. Acknowledging your gratitude for how merciful and good He has been to you and your family. Give thanks with a grateful heart, give thanks to the Holy one. Come into his gates with thanksgiving. Psalms 100:4-5 says:

> *"Enter into his gates with thanksgiving, and into his courts with praise: be thankful unto him, and bless his name. For the LORD is good; his mercy is everlasting; and his truth endureth to all generations."*

Psalms 69:30 also says:

> *"I will praise the name of God with a song, and will magnify him with thanksgiving."*

Prayer and thanksgiving go hand in hand as we read in the following scriptures: Colossians 4:2:

> *"Continue in prayer, and watch in the same with thanksgiving;"*

> *"Be careful for nothing; but in everything by prayer and supplication with thanksgiving let your requests be made known unto God."*
>
> Philippians 4:6

> *"Saying, Amen: Blessing, and glory, and wisdom, and thanksgiving, and honour, and power, and might, be unto our God for ever and ever. Amen."*
>
> Revelations 7:12

> *"And out of them shall proceed thanksgiving and the voice of them that make merry: and I will multiply them, and they shall not be few; I will also glorify them, and they shall not be small."*
>
> Jeremiah 30:19

> *"O give thanks unto the LORD; for he is good;*

for his mercy endureth for ever."
I Chronicles 16:34

We should magnify God and bless Him for all that He has done, continues to do and will yet do in our lives and the lives of our children on a daily basis.

Thanksgiving should not just be once a year but every day. We are grateful for countries that recognize that it is important to set a day apart as a national day for the people to say thanks and appreciate their Creator, say thanks to one another and appreciate what others do for them.

When we wake up in the morning, we have a reason to give thanks to God because many people slept the night before, but did not wake up the next day. Every opportunity we get, we should give thanks. We are to give thanks in good times and in bad times. When we have plenty, we are to be grateful and whenever we are going through trials and tribulations also we should learn to give thanks because all things work together for our good according to the word of God in Romans 8:28:

> *"And we know that all things work together for good to them that love God, to them who are the called according to his purpose."*

When we are full of thanksgiving for what God has done for us, He will do more. Just as in the natural, when we are grateful for what people have done for us they are encouraged to do more.

PRAYER OF PRAISE AND WORSHIP

Extol God for who He is. He is the Creator of heaven and earth. The air we breathe and everything around us were created by God in Genesis Chapter 1. Bow down and worship Him because he has all the power and ability to do all things. When you have done all that you know to do in prayer and you do not know what else to do; praise and worship God. When you have prayed and it seems nothing is working that is when you leave every need that you have in the hands of the Lord, and just worship and praise the King of Glory in reckless abandon.

Trust God to meet your needs because he knows even before you ask him and just worship. In worship you are telling God he is bigger than your problems, and that you trust that he is able to deliver you. In worship you are not asking for anything but simply loving on God and telling him how good He is to you and your family, how faithful He has been to you, how merciful He is and how grateful you are that He is in your life. Psalm 138:2 says:

> *"I will worship toward thy holy temple, and*
> *praise thy name for thy lovingkindness and*
> *for thy truth: for thou hast magnified thy word*
> *abovethy name."*

Worship is all about God and who He is: He is the centre of your focus. How wonderful will it be if we just come before Him not asking for anything, but to praise and worship Him for who He is.

When I just worship God either in my own words, in singing, dancing or listening to worship songs and sing along, He fights my battles and gives me victory even without praying for them. You can keep worship CDs in your car, bedroom and have it playing in your house and it will change the atmosphere in that house or in the car as you are driving to work, coming back home or running errands.

Praise is a weapon of warfare! God inhabits the praises of his people. Worship takes you into the inner court, before the throne of grace to find help in time of need. When you worship God you are not thinking about yourself, all your attention is on Him. Psalm 150:1-2 says:

> *"Praise ye the LORD. Praise God in his sanctuary: praise him in the firmament of his power. Praise him for his mighty acts: praise him according to his excellent greatness."*

The Father is looking for true worshippers who will worship him in spirit and in truth. John 4:23 tells us:

> *"But the hour cometh, and now is, when the true worshippers shall worship the Father in spirit and in truth: for the Father seeketh such to worship him."*

In praise however, you are thanking and acknowledging him for what he has done in your life. You look back at what he has done before and you are persuaded that he will do it again. Psalm 147:1 says:

> *"Praise ye the LORD: for it is good to sing praises unto our God; for it is pleasant; and praise is comely."*

You look at what He has done in some other person's life, and you are encouraged that if He did it for them surely He will do the same for you. This is why it is encouraged that we listen to people's testimonies of what God has done in their lives. Psalm 150:6 says:

> *"Let everything that hath breath praise the LORD. Praise ye the LORD."*

In 2 Chronicles 20:21 we are also told:

> *"And when he had consulted with the people,*

he appointed singers unto the LORD, and that should praise the beauty of holiness, as they went out before the army, and to say, Praise the LORD; for his mercy endureth for ever."

In the Old testament praise singers were appointed to go before the people and lead worship to God even as they bring their offerings. Today our praise and worship is important to God even as we give tithes and offerings. We see this fact hold true in the following scriptures:

Nehemiah 12:46 says

"For in the days of David and Asaph of old there were chief of the singers, and songs of praise and thanksgiving unto God."

"And all the congregation worshipped, and the singers sang, and the trumpeters sounded: and all this continued until the burnt offering was finished."

Chronicles 29:28

Luke 24:52-53 tells us that the early Christians worshipped and praised God after they witness Jesus taken up to heaven.

"And they worshipped Him, and returned to Jerusalem with great joy, and were continually in the temple praising and blessing God. Amen." (NKIV)

PRAYER OF SUPPLICATION

Supplication is when we cry out fervently to the Lord who is our strength and our redeemer. Pray prayer of supplication for all saints as in Ephesians 6:18:

"Praying always with all prayer and supplication in the Spirit, and watching thereunto with all perseverance and supplication for all saints;"

Supplication is entreating God to intervene in our needs and our deepest heart's desire. An example is where King Solomon prayed in 1 Kings 8:54 and others as follows:

"And it was so, that when Solomon had made an end of praying all this prayer and supplication unto the LORD, he arose from before the altar of the LORD, from kneeling on his knees with his hands spread up to heaven."

Psalm 119:170:

"Let my supplication come before thee: deliver me according to thy word."

We are encouraged to pray the prayer of supplication for ourselves in Philippians 4:6

"Be careful for nothing; but in everything by prayer and supplication with thanksgiving let your requests be made known unto God."

"These all continued with one accord in prayer and supplication, with the women, and Mary the mother of Jesus, and with his brethren."
                                                                Acts 1:14

"The LORD hath heard my supplication; the LORD will receive my prayer."
                                                                Psalm 6:9

We are to bring our strong reasons to God through supplication. God will hear us. We are counseled in Isaiah 41:21 to *"Produce your cause, saith the LORD; bring forth your strong reasons, saith the King of Jacob."*

Isaiah 1:18 also says:

> *"Come now, and let us reason together, saith the LORD: though your sins be as scarlet, they shall be as white as snow; though they be red like crimson, they shall be as wool."*

Do you have a reason why God should answer your prayer? Is it because you have been a doer of his word? Is it because it is your covenant promise from God? Is it because you pay your tithes? Is it because you have been faithful? Well, bring it! God is willing to reason with you.

Say the prayer of supplication for all in 1 Timothy 2:1-2:

> *"Therefore I exhort first for all that supplications, prayers, intercessions, and giving of thanks be made for all men, for kings and all who are in authority, that we may lead a quiet and peaceable life in all godliness and reverence."*

We are to pray for laborers to be sent into God's harvest in a prayer of supplication that is urgent, fervent and full of compassion for souls in Matthew 9:37-38:

> *"Then He said to His disciples, the harvest truly is plentiful, but the laborers are few. Therefore pray the Lord of the harvest to send out laborers into His harvest." (NKJV).*

We are to pray for the rain of God's spirit to be poured on our congregation, meetings all over the world and upon the earth. The following scriptures show where David confronted Goliath, when the latter defied the God of Israel. Is there not a cause (reason) why we should challenge the enemy? Is the devil tormenting us or buffeting our body with sickness and diseases? Are people asking us where is our God? Is the devil attacking our bodies, our marriage, our children or families? That is a "cause" right there. Let us go after the enemy in prayer in the name of the Lord like David did, and God will give us victory.

1 Sam 17:29, 45-46 tell us:

> *"And David said, What have I now done? Is there not a cause?"*

> *"Then said David to the Philistine, Thou comest to me with a sword, and with a spear, and with a shield: but I come to thee in the name of the LORD of hosts, the God of the armies of Israel, whom thou hast defied. This day will the LORD deliver thee into mine hand; and I will smite thee, and take thine head from thee; and I will give the carcasses of the host of the Philistines this day unto the fowls of the air, and to the wild beasts of the earth; that all the earth may know that there is a God in Israel."*

UNITED PRAYER

Hebrews 10:23-25 helps us to understand the importance of the Bible injunction concerning united prayer. It says:

> *"Let us hold fast the confession of our hope without wavering, for He who promised is faithful. And let us consider one another in order to stir up love and good works; Not forsaking the assembling of ourselves together, as is the manner of some, but exhorting one another, and so much the more as you see the Day approaching."*

Pray for one another. Praying with other children of God,

supporting one another and upholding one another in the faith. Testimonies are shared of victories God has given to some believers that will encourage another person going through the same thing or similar situation to know that they are not alone. That if God could come through for them surely God is no respecter of persons, their prayers will be answered too.

Strength comes from unity. A three-fold cord cannot easily be broken. It is important that we make conscious effort to attend weekly and Sunday services in our local churches or fellowships, so we can be partakers of united prayer. Acts 4:23-31 gives us an account of when Peter and John were imprisoned for preaching the gospel and healing the sick. When they were released they went to their own company, and raised their voices in prayer, praise and worshipped God. More souls were won to the Lord on that day and the faith of the other brethren was strengthened.

PRAYER OF CONSECRATION

This is the only time you pray Father, if it be thy will. It is a prayer where you have not made up your mind what you are about to do, but asking God to lead, guide, direct and strengthen you in the journey that He is asking you to undertake. Sometimes, it pertains to service in the Lord's vineyard, where you have to give yourself fully and completely to obey the will of God. It could be a decision has to be made that will change your life forever or affect your family members.

A prayer to consecrate and dedicate our lives to the service of God - to go anywhere and do anything that God will have us do – if it be thy will Oh Lord. An example is when Jesus was in the garden of Gethsemane in Luke 22:42:

"Saying, Father, if thou be willing, remove this cup from me: nevertheless not my will, but thine, be done."

100

The cup that our Lord and Savior was about to partake was heavy upon his shoulders and it was to take on the sins of the whole world, which will ultimately separate him from his Father because God cannot look upon sin. He is a holy God. Jesus Christ knew the purpose for which he was born (to save and redeem the world back unto God) so He knew he had to pay the price. Thank God that Jesus was obedient to the end to fulfill his destiny.

When praying for healing for example, you do not pray "if it be thy will" because the will of God concerning your healing is known in several scriptures in the Bible. 1 Peter 2:24 is one of them which says:

> *"Who his own self bare our sins in his own body on the tree, that we, being dead to sins, should live unto righteousness: by whose stripes ye were healed."*

God wants you healed so the prayer of consecration will not be appropriate at this time. The following scriptures are some of the evidences that tell us that God wants us healed.

> *"But unto you that fear my name shall the Sun of righteousness arise with healing in his wings; and ye shall go forth, and grow up as calves of the stall."*
>
> Malachi 4:2

> *"And Jesus went about all the cities and villages, teaching in their synagogues, and preaching the gospel of the kingdom, and healing every sickness and every disease among the people."*
>
> Matthew 9:35

> *"How God anointed Jesus of Nazareth with the Holy Ghost and with power: who went about*

doing good, and healing all that were oppressed of the devil; for God was with him."

Acts 10:38

We say the prayer of consecration sometimes when we have prayed against what we thought was the devil for so long, and nothing is happening. When we have fasted and prayed in agreement with friends and family members, when we have quoted the word of God and stood on the word for days, weeks and sometimes months and there is no answer from heaven then we say the prayer of consecration. We might need to back up and with humility ask God what his will is concerning the matter.

If we pray and fast and wait upon the Lord, he will speak to us. This happened to me many years ago. I was asking God to change a situation that was going to affect my life and that of my family, I prayed and fasted. I was binding and loosing. I did all the above and nothing happened. I then asked God for his will to be done and asked him for signs too! In his infinite mercy He showed me signs that made it crystal clear to me what He wanted me to do and I did.

The blessing of God came when I obeyed. Glory be to God. If it be thy will prayer is when you have not heard from God and you do not know what to do and it is not expressly written in His word what you are to do in that situation. But where God's will is known, all you need do is obey the word of God.

PRAYER OF COMMITMENT

This is a prayer you say when we want to commit our ways or our children into the hands of the Lord. We know that whatever we commit to God is safe, protected and preserved. This is when we cast all our care upon the Lord in prayer because we know He cares.

PRAYER IN THE SPIRIT: PRAYING IN TONGUES

Praying in the Spirit or praying with other tongues is where the Spirit of God helps us to pray. He is the one that gives us utterance. There are so many benefits to praying in the Spirit. I Corinthians 14:14-15 says we are to pray and sing in the spirit and in our understanding, for when we pray in tongues our spirit prays but our understanding is unfruitful. Romans 8:26 tells us:

> *"Likewise the Spirit also helps in our weaknesses. For we do not know what we should pray for as we ought, but the Spirit Himself makes intercession for us with groanings which cannot be uttered."*

We pray in the spirit to edify ourselves the Bible says in 1 Corinthians 14:4. Praying in the Spirit helps you to build up yourself on your most holy faith (Jude 20). And there is a rest that comes when we pray in the Holy Spirit as the prophet said in Isaiah 28:11-12

> *"For with stammering lips and another tongue He will speak to this people, to whom He said, "This is the rest with which you may cause the weary to rest," And, "This is the refreshing"; yet they would not hear."*

There is surely a rest that comes when we allow the Holy Spirit to help us in the place of prayer. He knows the heart and will of God concerning us, knows what to pray and can locate the problem better than we can. We cannot do without the Holy Spirit.

10

WHY SALVATION?

No one is righteous. Isaiah 64:6 says:

"But we are all as an unclean thing, and all our righteousness are as filthy rags; and we all do fade as a leaf; and our iniquities, like the wind, have taken us away."

The Creator of heaven and earth is a righteous God. In order to fellowship with Him, we have to accept the grace that is through believing in His Son Jesus Christ who came to die for us, so that we can have that communion with Him here on earth and have eternal life as well when we die.

When God created man in the Garden of Eden he had fellowship with God until sin came through disobedience. Jesus Christ came to earth so He could pay the price to redeem us back to that rightful place of fellowship with the Father that Adam and Eve lost to Satan in the book of Genesis. It is by grace that we are saved. It is a free gift from God.

> *"I call heaven and earth to record this day against you, that I have set before you life and death, blessing and cursing: therefore choose life, that both thou and thy seed may live:"*
>
> Deuteronomy 30:19

We have the responsibility to receive that gift in order to be saved. We receive the gift by believing on the Lord Jesus Christ that He was born, crucified, died, was buried and on the third day rose from the dead. He is alive and seated at the right hand of the Father, interceding for the saints. Salvation is available to everyone. Whosoever desires the gift, can receive it today by simply asking Jesus to come into their hearts and make Him their Lord and Savior. Ezekiel 18:23 says:

> *"Do I have any pleasure at all that the wicked should die? says the Lord God, and not that he should turn from his ways and live?"*

God is not interested that anyone should die but rather that all should live. The Bible says:

> *"For all have sinned and come short of the glory of God."*
>
> Romans 3:23

Therefore we all need a savior.

> *"For God so loved the world that He gave His only begotten Son, that whoever believes in Him should not perish but have everlasting life."*
>
> John 3:16

Salvation is God's grace by which we receive forgiveness for our sins when we confess them, repent and are forgiven, we stand before God as though we have never sinned. It is a free gift that has been paid for by the precious blood of our Lord and Savior Jesus Christ on the cross of Calvary.

> *"Therefore, if anyone is in Christ, he is a new creation: old things have passed away; behold all things have become new."*
>
> 2 Corinthians 5:17

> *"As the deer pants for the waterbrooks, so pants my soul for you O God. My soul thirsts for God, for the living God. When shall I come and appear before God?"*
>
> Psalms 42;1-2

There is a void or hunger in every human heart that only God is big enough to fill. Many have tried to fill this void with worldly things and pleasures but still come short of finding peace. For us to receive the gift of salvation we have to acknowledge that we are sinners. (Romans 3:23)

We need to confess our sins, everyone of them that we remember. I John 1:9 says:

> *"If we confess our sins, he is faithful and just to forgive us our sins, and to cleanse us from all unrighteousness."*

After confessing our sins, we need to repent according to Acts 3:19:

> *"Repent therefore, and be converted, that your sins may be blotted out, so that times of refreshing may come from the presence of the Lord."*

It is important that we forsake our sins and not hold on to them. Isaiah 55:7 says:

> *"Let the wicked forsake his way, and the unrigh-teous man his thoughts: and let him return unto the Lord, and he will have mercy on him; and to our God, for He will abundantly pardon."*

Believe that God is able to save you and deliver you according to his word in John 3:16 quoted earlier.

Take the above steps and pray aloud:

PRAYER

"Father, I acknowledge that I am a sinner, I repent of all my sins and I ask you to forgive me of all my sins and trespasses. Lord I believe that Jesus died for my sins, was buried and raised from the dead the third day. Come into my heart and be my Lord and Savior in Jesus name! Take control of my life from today. Thank you for saving me."

If you have prayed that prayer sincerely from your heart, God is faithful, He will save your soul. Congratulations, you are now in the family of God.

11

WHY SANCTIFICATION?

Sanctification is subsequent to salvation and it is a work of grace whereby we are made holy. Sanctification is a process whereby you consecrate yourself and you consciously live a life that is surrendered to God and living a life that is pleasing to Him. It is a daily walk in obedience to the word of God.

Being holy and living a life of holiness is not a walk in the part and neither is it a 100 meters dash, it is an enduring walk of love and obedience with the Lord daily. We have to die to our flesh, desires and wants daily, be consecrated, watchful and totally depend on the help of the Holy Spirit to walk in the spirit 365 days in the year. We have to be quick to repent, quick to forgive, have clean hands, study and meditate on the word of God daily so we know and are reminded daily what God expects of us so that we will not sin against Him.

When we do these things we will love God more and think more like God. Talk more and act more like Jesus would. When we receive Christ as our Lord and Savior, instantly our spirit man is regenerated, however, our body and soul is not transformed. We have an obligation to consciously work on these two through God's help. Romans 12:2 says:

>*"And be not conformed to this world: but be ye transformed by the renewing of your mind, that ye may prove what is that good, and acceptable, and perfect, will of God."*

After salvation we have to pray to God to sanctify us, and we have to daily read the word, be a doer of the word that we read or hear, in order for our mind to be renewed. We have a duty to renew our mind with the word of God daily. As we do, we should be conscious that old things are passed away and everything has become new in our lives. We have to study the word to know who God is and what He requires of us. It is just like when you are in a relationship with someone, you have to study the person, know what he/she likes and dislikes. Know what makes he/she happy, and what they dislike.

Normally, if we love someone we will not want to offend them. Same thing with our God, if we say we love God, we will not deliberately sin and offend Him. We have to read the word of God to know what He likes and what He does not like, so we will not sin against Him. Psalms 119:11 says:

>*"Thy word have I hid in mine heart, that I might not sin against thee."*

We find an example of someone whose mind was not

renewed after salvation in Acts 8:18-20:

> *"And when Simon saw that through laying on of*
> *the apostles' hands the Holy Ghost was given,*
> *he offered them money, Saying, Give me also this*
> *power, that on whomsoever I lay hands, he may*
> *receive the Holy Ghost. But Peter said unto him,*
> *Thy money perish with thee, because thou hast*
> *thought that the gift of God may be purchased*
> *with money."*

This is the story of one Simon who was a sorcerer. When he heard the word of God preached, he believed, but because his mind was not renewed, when hands were laid on people and they received the baptism of the Holy Ghost with the evidence of speaking in tongues, and he saw the demonstration of the power of God, he wanted to pay them in order to receive the gift so he could commercialize it. God is holy and He wants us to be holy. John 17:15-21:

> *"I pray not that thou shouldest take them out*
> *of the world, but that thou shouldest keep them*
> *from the evil. They are not of the world, even as*
> *I am not of the world. Sanctify them through thy*
> *truth: thy word is truth. As thou hast sent me into*
> *the world, even so have I also sent them into the*
> *world. And for their sakes I sanctify myself, that*
> *they also might be sanctified through the truth.*
> *Neither pray I for these alone, but for them also*
> *which shall believe on me through their word;*
> *That they all may be one; as thou, Father, art in*
> *me, and I in thee, that they also may be one in*
> *us: that the world may believe that thou hast sent*
> *me."*

Our sanctification has been paid for, we can live a holy life through the finished work of our Lord and Savior. The

Word of God sanctifies us. Jesus is our Sanctifier. Hebrews 13:12 says:

> *"Jesus also, that he might sanctify the people with his own blood, suffered without the gate."*

> *"For by one offering he hath perfected forever them that are sanctified"*
> Hebrews 10:14

By the sacrifice of Jesus on the cross we are sanctified. We are sanctified by the word of God and Ephesians 5:26-27 says:

> *"That he might sanctify and cleanse it with the washing of water by the word, That he might present it to himself a glorious church, not having spot, or wrinkle, or any such thing; but that it should be holy and without blemish."*

We have a part to play, and that responsibility is to consciously live our lives through the help of the Spirit of God. We cannot go about saying we are sinners, but rather we have been saved by grace and are required to walk in holiness. We are to walk out our salvation with fear and trembling. The fear the Bible is talking about here is reverence for the word of God, and taking heed to doing the word, so that we do not deliberately sin daily just like an unbeliever would.

And if we do fall into sin, we have an advocate with the Father, Jesus Christ the righteous who is always interceding on our behalf. We are to jealously watch our mouth-gate, eye-gate, and ear-gate. We have to watch what comes out of our mouth (what we say) watch what we feed our eyes on (what we look/gaze at) and what we hear (what we listen to). Faith comes by hearing and hearing by the word of God. So also doubt or fear comes by hearing and hearing by negative words from the enemy of our soul.

If we want to live holy we have a responsibility to walk in the light of God's word. If it were not possible God will not demand it of us. There are so many distractions all around us but we can do all things through Christ. The grace of God is sufficient.

12

WHY THE BAPTISM IN THE HOLY SPIRIT?

After we are born again and are set apart for the Lord, we need the infusion of power from on high with the evidence of speaking in tongues as the spirit gives utterance. Ye shall receive power after the Holy Ghost is come upon you, to speak the word of God with boldness, to serve, live victoriously, do miracles and wonders, and witness for God.

Some people receive salvation and the baptism in the Holy Spirit the same time. We were taught to tarry at the altar, and have other believers pray us through till we received our baptism. You can receive it by the laying on of hands. You can receive it as you pray and ask God to baptize you with the Holy Spirit.

The Christian life is not supposed to be a struggle. We need oil to lubricate our lives so we can function with ease. To receive the Holy Spirit the following scripture will help us know how and who can receive the Holy Spirit. The baptism of the Holy Spirit is for all believers not just for a select few. It is a gift from God. We have to receive it just as we received salvation by faith in Jesus Christ. Prophesies about the baptism of the Holy Spirit were given in Isaiah 28:11 which says:

"For with stammering lips and another tongue will he speak to this people."

The Holy Spirit was promised in the Old Testament in Joel 2:28-29:

"And it shall come to pass afterward, that I will pour out my spirit upon all flesh; and your sons and your daughters shall prophesy, your old men shall dream dreams, your young men shall see visions: And also upon the servants and upon the handmaids in those days will I pour out my spirit."

"And when the day of Pentecost was fully come, they were all with one accord in one place. And suddenly there came a sound from heaven as of a rushing mighty wind, and it filled all the house where they were sitting. And there appeared unto them cloven tongues like as of fire, and it sat upon each of them. And they were all filled with the Holy Ghost, and began to speak with other tongues, as the Spirit gave them utterance."

Acts 2:1-4

The baptism of the Holy Spirit was promised by our Lord Jesus Christ. He is the Comforter. Acts 2:33 says:

116

"Therefore being by the right hand of God exalted, and having received of the Father the promise of the Holy Ghost, he hath shed forth this, which ye now see and hear."

People received the gift by the laying on of hands. Acts 9:17:

"And Ananias went his way, and entered into the house; and putting his hands on him said, Brother Saul, the Lord, even Jesus, that appeared unto thee in the way as thou camest, hath sent me, that thou mightest receive thy sight, and be filled with the Holy Ghost."

Others received while the word of God was being spoken, they believed in their hearts and the power of God fell on them.

"While Peter yet spake these words, the Holy Ghost fell on all them which heard the word. And they of the circumcision which believed were astonished, as many as came with Peter, because that on the Gentiles also was poured out the gift of the Holy Ghost."

Acts 10:44-45

Mark 16:17 says:

"...these signs will follow those that believe. In My name they will cast out demons, they will speak with new tongues."

Miracles, signs and wonders happen through the power of the Holy Spirit and Acts 8:5-8 says:

"Then Philip went down to the city of Samaria, and preached Christ unto them. And the people with one accord gave heed unto those things

117

which Philip spake, hearing and seeing the miracles which he did. For unclean spirits, crying with loud voice, came out of many that were possessed with them: and many taken with palsies, and that were lame, were healed. And there was great joy in that city."

Furthermore, we also read in Acts 8:12-21 the following revealed words:

"But when they believed Philip preaching the things concerning the kingdom of God, and the name of Jesus Christ, they were baptized, both men and women. Then Simon himself believed also: and when he was baptized, he continued with Philip, and wondered, beholding the miracles and signs which were done. Now when the apostles which were at Jerusalem heard that Samaria had received the word of God, they sent unto them Peter and John: Who, when they were come down, prayed for them, that they might receive the Holy Ghost: they were baptized in the name of the Lord Jesus. (For as yet he was fallen upon none of them: only Then laid they their hands on them, and they received the Holy Ghost. And when Simon saw that through laying on of the apostles' hands the Holy Ghost was given, he offered them money, Saying, Give me also this power, that on whomsoever I lay hands, he may receive the Holy Ghost. But Peter said unto him, Thy money perish with thee, because thou hast thought that the gift of God may be purchased with money. Thou hast neither part nor lot in this matter: for thy heart is not right in the sight of God."

Our hearts have to be right before God to receive the Holy Spirit. We can receive the Holy Spirit by the laying on of hands. The spirit of prophesy comes with the baptism of the Holy Spirit as we read in Acts 19:3-6:

"And he said unto them, Unto what then were ye baptized? And they said, Unto John's baptism. Then said Paul, John verily baptized with the baptism of repentance, saying unto the people, that they should believe on him which should come after him, that is, on Christ Jesus. When they heard this, they were baptized in the name of the Lord Jesus. And when Paul had laid his hands upon them, the Holy Ghost came on them; and they spake with tongues, and prophesied."

Also in I Corinthians 14:1-18, 39 we read:

"Follow after charity, and desire spiritual gifts, but rather that ye may prophesy. For he that speaketh in an unknown tongue speaketh not unto men, but unto God: for no man understandeth him; howbeit in the spirit he speaketh mysteries. But he that prophesieth speaketh unto men to edification, and exhortation, and comfort. He that speaketh in an unknown tongue edifieth himself; but he that prophesieth edifieth the church. I would that ye all spake with tongues, but rather that ye prophesied: for greater is he that prophesieth than he that speaketh with tongues, except he interpret, that the church may receive edifying. Now, brethren, if I come unto you speaking with tongues, what shall I profit you, except I shall speak to you either by revelation, or by knowledge, or by prophesying, or by doctrine? And even things without life giving sound, whether pipe or harp, except they give a distinction in the sounds, how shall it be known what is piped or harped? For if the trumpet give an uncertain

sound, who shall prepare himself to the battle? So likewise ye, except ye utter by the tongue words easy to be understood, how shall it be known what is spoken? for ye shall speak into the air. There are, it may be, so many kinds of voices in the world, and none of them is without signification. Therefore if I know not the meaning of the voice, I shall be unto him that speaketh a barbarian, and he that speaketh shall be a barbarian unto me. Even so ye, for as much as ye are zealous of spiritual gifts, seek that ye may excel to the edifying of the church.

Wherefore let him that speaketh in an unknown tongue pray that he may interpret.

For if I pray in an unknown tongue, my spirit prayeth, but my understanding is unfruitful.

What is it then? I will pray with the spirit, and I will pray with the understanding also: I will sing with the spirit, and I will sing with the understanding also. Else when thou shalt bless with the spirit, how shall he that occupieth the room of the unlearned say Amen at thy giving of thanks, seeing he understandeth not what thou sayest? For thou verily givest thanks well, but the other is not edified. I thank my God, I speak with tongues more than ye all:"

The Apostle Paul is not saying that we should not desire to speak in tongues or receive the gift of the baptism of the Holy Spirit, but rather that we should ask God for the ability to interpret tongues as well. That way if we edify ourselves, and speak mysteries when we pray in tongues, when we interpret what we have said in other language other people can understand, and they will be edified.

We are able to pray longer when we pray in tongues and also able to cover many areas in the spirit realm as the spirit of God gives us utterance on what to pray. I Corinthians 14:39 says:

> *"Wherefore, brethren, covet to prophesy, and forbid not to speak with tongues."*

For there are some that believe tongues are of the devil or speaking in tongues has ended or ceased with the Disciples. Speaking in tongues is for today, glory be to God, and it has its benefits to the individual and to the Church. John 14:16-17, 26 says:

> *"And I will pray the Father, and he shall give you another Comforter, that he may abide with you for ever; Even the Spirit of truth; whom the world cannot receive, because it seeth him not, neither knoweth him: but ye know him; for he dwelleth with you, and shall be in you. But the Comforter, which is the Holy Ghost, whom the Father will send in my name, he shall teach you all things, and bring all things to your remembrance, whatsoever I have said unto you."*

Acts 1:5-8 says:

> *"For John truly baptized with water; but ye shall be baptized with the Holy Ghost not many days hence. When they therefore were come together, they asked of him, saying, Lord, wilt thou at this time restore again the kingdom to Israel? And he said unto them, It is not for you to know the times or the seasons, which the Father hath put in his own power. But ye shall receive power, after that the Holy Ghost is come upon you: and ye shall be witnesses unto me both in Jerusalem, and in all Judaea, and in Samaria, and unto the uttermost part of the earth."*

PRAYER

Pray: **"Father in the name of Jesus, I ask you to baptize me today with power and the evidence of speaking in other tongues as the Spirit gives me utterance. Give me POWER to do the works that God has called me to do on earth. I receive your gift O Lord in Jesus name. Amen."**

Open your mouth, begin to speak and praise His name.

13

WHAT ROLE DOES THE SPEAKING WITH OTHER TONGUES PLAY IN PRAYER?

Praying is the Spirit which is the same as praying with other tongues (I don't mean you praying in your mother tongue if you are in the midst of people who do not speak your native language) is very important in our prayer life. It helps us to pray the will of God in prayer. It directly links us to the spiritual realm where we are not looking for words or trying to form a sentence in prayer, but instead we can connect/depend on the Spirit of God to give us utterance. Sometimes we know not how to pray as we ought to, but the Spirit groans in intercession on our behalf and gives us utterance as we read in Romans 8:26 says:

"Likewise the Spirit also helpeth our infirmities: for we know not what we should pray for as we ought: but the Spirit itself maketh intercession for us with groanings which cannot be uttered."

When we pray in our understanding we easily run out of words, but when we pray in the Holy Spirit, we are able to pray for hours as we pray mysteries from heaven. We are able to tap into the heavenly realm and pray things that are yet to come/in the future; we pray the heart of the Father because we are not praying in our intellect but depending on God to give us what to pray.

We are able to pray for the needs of others without having an idea what they are going through, but the Spirit of God who knows all things will pray through us what prayers the people need. You end up confusing the devil and his demons because they do not understand what you are praying and we are able to bypass the natural and move into the realm of the supernatural. 1 Corinthians 14:2 tells us:

"For he that speaketh in an unknown tongue speaketh not unto men, but unto God: for no man understandeth him; howbeit in the spirit he speaketh mysteries."

However, the Bible warns us that if we speak in tongues and have no love towards our neighbor, we are like sounding brass. 1 Corinthians 13:1 says:

"Though I speak with the tongues of men and of angels, and have not charity, I am become as sounding brass, or a tinkling cymbal."

Walking in love at all times helps our prayers to be answered.

14

WHAT DOES OBEDIENCE HAVE TO DO WITH ANSWERED PRAYER?

Obedience is the willingness to do what God requires of us. It is when we humble ourselves to do what pleases the Father. It is not our agenda, but what does the word of God say concerning the matter we are faced with that is important. We must resolve to completely surrender and reverence God. If we are living a life of obedience to the word of God, it is easier for our prayers to be answered as we read in Psalms 24:3-5:

> *"Who shall ascend into the hill of the LORD? or who shall stand in his holy place?*
> *He that hath clean hands, and a pure heart; who hath not lifted up his soul unto vanity, nor sworn deceitfully. He shall receive the blessing from the*

*LORD, and righteousness from the God of his
salvation."*

I Samuel 15:22 says:

> *"And Samuel said, Hath the LORD as great
> delight in burnt offerings and sacrifices, as in
> obeying the voice of the LORD? Behold, to obey
> is better than sacrifice, and to hearken than the
> fat of rams."*

This means that God would rather prefer we are doers of
His word than we bringing a huge offering into the church.
Obedience to the word of God is key to answered prayers.
We are told to forgive our enemies so that our sins might
be forgiven us in Mark 11:25

> *"And when ye stand praying, forgive, if ye have
> ought against any: that your Father also which is
> in heaven may forgive you your trespasses."*

Isaiah 1:19a says:

> *"If ye be willing and obedient, ye shall eat the
> good of the land:"*

If we are willing and obedient in following after God and
doing his will, we will be prosperous wherever we go. Our
prayer should always be: **"Lord, please help me to be
willing in heart and obedient to do as your word says
in the name of Jesus!"**

Obedience which is synonymous with having a perfect
heart toward God helps our prayers to be answered more
quickly as we see in 2 Chronicles 16:9:

> *"For the eyes of the LORD run to and fro
> throughout the whole earth, to show himself*

strong in the behalf of them whose heart is perfect toward him."

And also in Proverbs 21:3 we read:

"To do righteousness and justice is more acceptable to the Lord than sacrifice". (NKJV)

The story of Naaman the leper is an example of what obedience does. He was healed when he obeyed the simple instruction given by Prophet Elisha to go and dip in the muddy river Jordan seven times. At first he was arrogant, and felt he should have been told to go and wash in a cleaner river in Damascus, but his servant prevailed on him and he obeyed (2 Kings 5:1-14). When we are obedient to the word of God, we will receive our breakthroughs and prayers answered.

The widow of Zarephath is another example of obedience. The man of God asked her to go, and bake him a cake first and then bake for her family with the remaining flour she had left in the house for famine was raging in the land. She could have argued that the man of God was greedy, and does not care for her and her child, but she obeyed the man of God. That simple obedience led to a great miracle that not only fed her and her son, but sustained her and her household throughout the time of famine in the land (1 Kings 17:10-16).

We thank God for the sacrifice of our Lord and Savior, Jesus Christ for through his obedience we are made righteous. We all became sinners through Adam's disobedience. Romans 5:19 says:

"For as by one man's disobedience many were made sinners, so by the obedience of one shall many be made righteous."

God is not interested in our sacrifice, He is interested in our obedience. Man is moved/impressed by outward appearance but God is interested in the motives of your heart.

15

HOW LONG SHOULD YOU PRAY ABOUT A PARTICULAR THING?

It is interesting to note that when you first give your life to Christ or became born again, the moment you prayed for something your prayers were answered. When you prayed for a particular spot to park at the mall, or wherever we were going, a spot was miraculously available for you to park, but as time goes on in your Christian walk, you find that sometime you have to fast and pray for a longer period before you receive an answer to your prayers.

Could it be that the child like faith you had is not being stirred up now that you have been born again for a long period? Or could it be that you are not praying with the same expectation like you used to have? Do you still believe that God can do whatever you ask of Him? Jesus Christ said that whatever we ask the Father in His name it shall be given unto us. Our response or answers to prayer can be immediate and sometimes it might take a longer period for us to see the manifestation of the answered prayer. The moment we pray God hears us as we read in Mark 11:22-24:

"And Jesus answering saith unto them, Have faith in God. For verily I say unto you, That whosoever shall say unto this mountain, Be thou removed, and be thou cast into the sea; and shall not doubt in his heart, but shall believe that those things which he saith shall come to pass; he shall have whatsoever he saith. Therefore I say unto you, What things soever ye desire, when ye pray, believe that ye receive them, and ye shall have them."

At times we have to be like the widow and the unjust judge, who would not let up after she had made her request known to the judge. She kept on persisting until the judge granted her request or if you like, until her manifestation came as it is revealed to us in Luke 18:1-7:

"And he spake a parable unto them to this end, that men ought always to pray, and not to faint; Saying, There was in a city a judge, which feared not God, neither regarded man: And there was a widow in that city; and she came unto him, saying, Avenge me of mine adversary. And he would not for a while: but afterward he said within himself, Though I fear not God, nor regard man; Yet because this widow troubleth me, I will avenge her, lest by her continual coming she weary me. And the Lord said, Hear what the unjust judge saith. And shall not God avenge his own elect, which cry day and night unto him, though he bear long with them?"

The persistence of the widow got her the victory she was seeking. We have to be persistent in prayer also. Persistence in praise, thanksgiving, worship, asking, seeking and knocking is a quality that will get our prayers answered.

Daniel prayed, and the moment he did his prayers were heard and the Bible tells us that the answer to his prayer was dispatched immediately, but the Prince of Persia withstood angel Gabriel who was bringing the miracle. He was held down for many days until angel Michael came to his rescue after he called for reinforcement. The manifestation of the prayer of Daniel came after the breakthrough.

So also we have to learn that when our prayers are not answered, we do not give up. We have to examine ourselves that we are praying according to the will of God, and that we have no unforgiveness in our hearts towards anyone. God will perform His word.

Daniel 10:12-14 says:

> *"Then said he unto me, Fear not, Daniel: for from the first day that thou didst set thine heart to understand, and to chasten thyself before thy God, thy words were heard, and I am come for thy words. But the prince of the kingdom of Persia withstood me one and twenty days: but, lo, Michael, one of the chief princes, came to help me; and I remained there with the kings of Persia. Now I am come to make thee understand what shall befall thy people in the latter days: for yet the vision is for many days."*

It is important to note that there are times you pray and you receive a witness in your spirit that your prayer has been answered. In that situation you can begin to praise and thank God for the manifestation of the answer to your prayer. You want to be careful not to cancel what you have prayed by doubting if God will do it or not but rather remain in worship, praise and thanksgiving for as long as it takes for you to see your miracle. Open your mouth and declare that God is good and pull down every lie the enemy might want to whisper in your ears that God has not done it. Hold your ground in praise, worship and thanksgiving until you receive your blessing.

Furthermore, renew your mind with the word and God's promises at this time. Surround yourself with people who believe what you believe and will not speak doubt over you. Another good example of this is the woman in Matthew 15:22-28 who would not give up until her daughter was healed. She was not offended when called names, neither was she in a hurry. She was determined, and persistent till she received her blessing from the Lord as we read in the following passages:

> *"And, behold, a woman of Canaan came out*
> *of the same coasts, and cried unto him, saying,*
> *Have mercy on me, O Lord, thou Son of David;*
> *my daughter is grievously vexed with a devil.*
> *But he answered her not a word. And his dis-*
> *ciples came and besought him, saying, Send her*
> *away; for she crieth after us. But he answered*
> *and said, I am not sent but unto the lost sheep*
> *of the house of Israel. Then came she and wor-*
> *shipped him, saying, Lord, help me. But he an-*
> *swered and said, It is not meet to take the chil-*
> *dren's bread, and to cast it to dogs. And she said,*
> *Truth, Lord: yet the dogs eat of the crumbs which*
> *full from their masters' table. Then Jesus an*
> *swered and said unto her, O woman, great is thy*
> *faith: be it unto thee even as thou wilt. And her*
> *daughter was made whole from that very hour."*
>
> Matthew 15:22-28

Sometimes we have to wait upon the Lord for the answer to our prayers. Have faith, keep believing, praising and thanking Him for the manifestation of what we have asked for in prayer. Isaiah 40:28-31 says:

> *"Hast thou not known? Hast thou not heard, that the everlasting God, the LORD, the Creator of the ends of the earth, fainteth not, neither is weary? There is no searching of his understanding. He giveth power to the faint; and to them that have no might he increaseth strength. Even the youths shall faint and be weary, and the young men shall utterly fall: But they that wait upon the LORD shall renew their strength; they shall mount up with wings as eagles; they shall run, and not be weary; and they shall walk, and not faint." (KJV)*

When prayer and fasting is not yielding any result that we desired, back up and examine if you are not praying amiss, or if you are praying the will of God. If you have studied the word and found yourself in line with the word of God then wait patiently for your answer, with praise and thanksgiving. Isaiah 45:19 says God has not called Jacob to serve him in vain,

> *"I have not spoken in secret, in a darkplace of the earth: I said not unto the seed of Jacob,Seek ye me in vain: I the LORD speak righteousness, I declare things that are right."*

When we are faithful to serve God and teach our children to serve God, the blessing of God will be upon our lives and that of our descendants. He will answer our prayers in due season.

16

WHAT DOES FAITH HAVE TO DO WITH YOUR PRAYERS BEING ANSWERED?

Faith is putting our eyes upon Jesus without any doubt in our hearts. Faith is, believing in what you do not see, hear, feel or touch. You believe in the invisible, something that is not tangible, something that you are looking forward to but you do not yet have in your hands. Even though you do not see it, smell it, feel it or touch it, it is as real to you as though you had it in your hands. Faith also means having absolute trust in God and what He has said in his word. Faith has a lot to do with our prayers being answered because without faith in God we cannot receive anything from Him. Romans 1:17:

*"For therein is the righteousness of God re-
vealed from faith to faith: as it is written, The just
shall live by faith."*

When we have faith in God, we are saying to Him we trust
that you are able to deliver on what you have promised.
James 1:6-7 says:

*"But let him ask in faith, nothing wavering. For
he that wavers is like a wave of the sea driven
with the wind and tossed. For let not that man
think that he shall receive any thing of the Lord."
(KJV)*

It is by faith that we are healed in the name of Jesus Christ.
As we read in Acts 3:16:

*"And his name through faith in his name hath
made this man strong, whom ye see and know:
yea, the faith which is by him hath given him this
perfect soundness in the presence of you all."*

We are justified by faith and not by our works as we see in
Galatians 2:16:

*"Knowing that a man is not justified by the works
of the law, but by the faith of Jesus Christ, even
we have believed in Jesus Christ, that we might
be justified by the faith of Christ, and not by the
works of the law: for by the works of the law
shall no flesh be justified."*

The book of Hebrews is referred to by many as the Hall
of fame of Faith because we see many men and woman
who walked with God, and what distinguished them was
their faith in God. Through their absolute trust in God,
they were able to move mountains, do exploits, tell the sun
to stand still while battles were being fought, commanded

136

fire to fall from heaven, raised the dead, and performed many miracles. These were men and women just like us, but what distinguished them was their faith, absolute trust in God and their prayers. Hebrews 11:1-3 says:

"Now faith is the substance of things hoped for, the evidence of things not seen. For by it the elders obtained a good report. Through faith we understand that the worlds were framed by the word of God, so that things which are seen were not made of things which do appear."

Also Hebrews 11:6 then goes on to say:

"But without faith it is impossible to please him: for he that cometh to God must believe that he is, and that he is a rewarder of them that diligently seek him."

Faith is what moves God, not our wants, or our needs, He hears our cries of faith. Do we believe that He can do what we are asking Him to do? That determines how soon and how effectively our prayers are answered. In confirming this fact, Mark 11:22-24 says:

"And Jesus answering saith unto them, Have faith in God. For verily I say unto you, That whosoever shall say unto this mountain, Be thou removed, and be thou cast into the sea; and shall not doubt in his heart, but shall believe that those things which he saith shall come to pass; he shall have whatsoever he saith. Therefore I say unto you, What things soever ye desire, when ye pray, believe that ye receive them, and ye shall have them."

Pray: **"Father, in the name of Jesus I rebuke every spirit of doubt and unbelief in my life. Help me to have**

faith in your ability to grant me the desires of my heart as I pray. Thank you God that I believe your word and I receive in Jesus name Amen."

Hearing the word of God preached in churches and synagogues, on radio, TV, CDs and all the other avenues by which we can hear the word of God today brings faith into our hearts. But be careful what you hear, when you listen to words that are positive, they will bring faith, likewise words that are negative will bring doubt into our hearts and minds. Therefore we have to be very sensitive to what we hear. Romans 10:17 says:

> *"So then faith cometh by hearing, and hearing by the word of God."*

When we read or hear people's testimonies of how God delivered them or answered their prayers they build faith in us which enables us to believe in our hearts that if God did it for them, He can do it for us also. We see in the following verses of scriptures how men and women of old had faith in God and believed that He was able to do what He said He would do. Hebrews 11:7-11 reveal to us that:

> *"By faith Noah, being warned of God of things not seen as yet, moved with fear, prepared an ark to the saving of his house; by the which he condemned the world, and became heir of the righteousness which is by faith. By faith Abraham, when he was called to go out into a place which he should after receive for an inheritance, obeyed; and he went out, not knowing whither he went. By faith he sojourned in the land of promise, as in a strange country, dwelling in tabernacles with Isaac and Jacob, the heirs with him of the same promise: For he looked for a city which hath foundations, whose builder and maker is God. Through faith also Sara herself received*

strength to conceive seed, and was delivered of a child when she was past age, because she judged him faithful who had promised."

The word of God says if we have faith as small as a mustard seed, we can move mountains if we do not have any doubts in our hearts. Also Matthew 17:20 declares:

"And Jesus said unto them, Because of your unbelief: for verily I say unto you, If ye have faith as a grain of mustard seed, ye shall say unto this mountain, Remove hence to yonder place; and it shall remove; and nothing shall be impossible unto you."

If we believe that God can do it, all things are possible. Luke 1:37 says: *"For with God nothing shall be impossible."* God has given each one of us a measure of faith as we read in Romans 12:3:

"For I say, through the grace given unto me, to every man that is among you, not to think of himself more highly than he ought to think; but to think soberly, according as God hath dealt to every man the measure of faith."

Faith in God plays an important role in prayer because when we have faith and do not doubt the ability of God, we are saying that God is bigger than our problems or challenges. But when we do not exercise faith in God when we pray we are saying that our problem is greater than God, and we are magnifying the situation instead of magnifying our Creator who is in control of all things.

Another example of faith is the woman with the issue of blood, who would not give up until she received from God believing that if she is able to touch the helm of Jesus' garment she shall be made whole as we read in Mark 5:25-34 says:

> *"And a certain woman, which had an issue of blood twelve years, And had suffered many things of many physicians, and had spent all that she had, and was nothing bettered, but rather grew worse, When she had heard of Jesus, came in the press behind, and touched his garment. For she said, If I may touch but his clothes, I shall be whole. And straightway the fountain of her blood was dried up; and she felt in her body that she was healed of that plague. And Jesus, immediately knowing in himself that virtue had gone out of him, turned him about in the press, and said, Who touched my clothes? And his disciples said unto him, Thou seest the multitude thronging thee, and sayest thou, Who touched me?*
> *And he looked round about to see her that had done this thing. But the woman fearing and trembling, knowing what was done in her, came and fell down before him, and told him all the truth. And he said unto her, Daughter, thy faith hath made thee whole; go in peace, and be whole of thy plague."*

We have to speak to our situation by faith in the word of God. Examples abound where Jesus Christ spoke to the sea to be calm, the fig tree to wither and die, Lazarus to rise up from the dead, etc. We have been given the authority to speak to situations and circumstances and command them to turn around, and let God be God in our lives. We have to release our faith in God so that the angels of God can go about doing their job – which is to hearken to the voice of His word.

We have to make up our mind to walk in faith and our prayers will be answered. Jesus is the author and finisher of our faith, we have to lay aside every doubt and be determined and dedicated to God. Hebrews 12:1-2 says:

> *"Wherefore seeing we also are compassed about with so great a cloud of witnesses, let us lay aside every weight, and the sin which doth so easily beset us, and let us run with patience the race that is set before us, Looking unto Jesus the author and finisher of our faith; who for the joy that was set before him endured the cross, despising the shame, and is set down at the right hand of the throne of God."*

REFERENCES

- Bible quotations were taken from the King James Version of the Bible

- Bible quotations were taken from The Amplified Version of the Bible

- Brother Kenneth E. Hagin, Rhema Bible Church, Tulsa, OK.

- Pastor Emiko Amotsuka, Lagos Nigeria

- The Official King James Bible Online (Authorized Version KJV)

- Higher Way Publication, Apostolic Faith Church, Portland, Oregon

- The Art of prayer by Kenneth E. Hagin, 1992 4th edition, Rhema Bible Church.

- The Threefold Nature of Man by Kenneth E. Hagin, 1973 2nd edition, Rhema Bible Church.